W9-ASQ-525

THE PROFESSIONAL SELLING SKILLS
WORKBOOK

THE PROFESSIONAL SELLING SKILLS
WORKBOOK

RAMON A. AVILA
BALL STATE UNIVERSITY

THOMAS N. INGRAM
COLORADO STATE UNIVERSITY

RAYMOND W. LAFORGE
UNIVERSITY OF LOUISVILLE

MICHAEL R. WILLIAMS
ILLINOIS STATE UNIVERSITY

The Dryden Press
Harcourt Brace College Publishers

Fort Worth   Philadelphia   San Diego   New York   Orlando   Austin   San Antonio
Toronto   Montreal   London   Sydney   Tokyo

Acquisitions Editor: Jim Lizotte
Developmental Editor: Paul Stewart
Project Editor: Jim Patterson
Art Director: Lora Knox
Production Manager: Jessica Wyatt
Art & Literary Rights Editor: Adele Krause
Product Manager: Lisé Johnson
Marketing Coordinator: Sam Stubblefield

Copyeditor: Carolyn Crabtree
Proofreader: Jody St. John
Text Type: 12/14 AGaramond

Copyright © 1996 by Harcourt Brace & Company

All rights reservrd. No part of this publication may be reproduced or transmitted in any form or by any means, electronic or mechanical, including photocopy, recording, or any information storage and retrieval system, without permission in writing from the publisher.

Although for mechanical reasons all pages of this publication are perforated, only those pages imprinted with a Harcourt Brace & Company copyright notice are intended for removal.

Requests for permission to make copies of any part of the work should be mailed to: Permissions Department, Harcourt Brace & Company, 6277 Sea Harbor Drive, Orlando, FL 32887-6777.

Address for orders:
The Dryden Press
6277 Sea Harbor Drive
Orlando, FL 32887-6777
1-800-782-4479, or 1-800-433-0001 (in Florida)

Address for editorial correspondence:
The Dryden Press
301 Commerce Street, Suite 3700
Fort Worth, TX 76102

ISBN: 0-03-016332-3

Credits appear on pages 261–262, which constitute a continuation of the copyright page.

Printed in the United States of America

5 6 7 8 9 0 1 2 3 4   0 6 6   9 8 7 6 5 4 3 2 1

The Dryden Press
Harcourt Brace College Publishers

THE DRYDEN PRESS SERIES IN MARKETING

Avila, Ingram, LaForge, and Williams
The Professional Selling Skills Workbook

Bateson
Managing Services Marketing: Text and Readings
Third Edition

Blackwell, Blackwell, and Talarzyk
Contemporary Cases in consumer Behavior
Fourth Edition

Boone and Kurtz
Contemporary Marketing Plus
Eighth Edition

Churchill
Marketing Research: Methodological Foundations
Sixth Edition

Czinkota and Ronkainen
Global Marketing

Czinkota and Romkainen
International Marketing
Fourth Edition

Czinkota and Ronkainen
International Marketing Strategy: Environmental Assessment and Entry Strategies

Dickson
Marketing Management

Engel, Blackwell, and Miniard
Consumer Behavior
Eighth Edition

Futrell
Sales Management
Fourth Edition

Grover
Theory & Simulation of Market-Focused Management

Ghosh
Retail Management
Second Edition

Hassan and Blackwell
Global Marketing: Managerial Dimensions and Cases

Hutt and Speh

Business Marketing Management: A Strategic View of Industrial and Organizational Markets
Fifth Edition

Ingram and LaForge
Sales Management: Analysis and Decision Making
Second Edition

Lewison
Marketing Management: An Overview

Lindgren and Shimp
Marketing: An Interactive Learning System

Krugman, Reid, Dunn, and Barban
Advertising: Its Role in Modern Marketing
Eighth Edition

Oberhaus, Ratliffe, and Stauble
Professional Selling: A Relationship Process
Second Edition

Parente, Vaden Bergh, Barban, and Marra
Advertising Campaign Strategy: A Guide to Marketing Communication Plans

Rachman
Marketing Today
Third Edition

Rosenbloom
Marketing Channels: A Management View
Fifth Edition

Schaffer
Applying Marketing Principles Software

Schellinck and Maddox
Marketing Research: A Computer-Assisted Approach

Schnaars
MICROSIM

Schuster and Copeland
Global Business: Planning for Sales and Negotiations

Shimp
Promotion Management and Marketing Communications
Third Edition

Talarzyk
Cases and Exercises in Marketing

Terpstra and Sarathy
International Marketing
Sixth Edition

Weitz and Wensley
Readings in Strategic Marketing Analysis, Planning, and Implementation

Zikmund
Exploring Marketing Research
Fifth Edition

HARCOURT BRACE COLLEGE OUTLINE SERIES

Peterson
Principles of Marketing

To Terry, Sarah, Anne, Ryan, Laura, and my parents

—Ramon Avila

To Jacque and my parents

—Tom Ingram

To Susan, Alexandra, Kelly, and my parents

—Buddy LaForge

To Marilyn, Aimee, Kerri, and my parents

—Mike Williams

PREFACE

Courses in professional selling focus on developing the understanding and ability to use the varied processes of interpersonal behavior and communication. Noting the applied nature of this subject matter, experienced instructors from both industry and academia stress the importance of minimizing the more traditional lecture and note taking class format. Instead, they recommend more active, high participation formats structured to provide more effective illustration and demonstration of the various principles and processes. Further, the experiential nature of this high participation format provides students with opportunities to practice the application of the principles and to further hone their selling skills.

Designed to bring excitement, practical experience, and an additional touch of realism into the selling class experience, *The Professional Selling Skills Workbook* was crafted to address the multiple needs of all participants. Students' conceptual organization is improved by grouping the individual exercises into concept modules. This organization of material plus the "stand-alone" format of each exercise allows students to maximize their class and study time—everything is in one place, all set-up, and ready to use. The students will have the complete set of exercises in their workbook which alleviates the frustration of keeping up with a multitude of individual handouts.

Students further benefit through participating in activities that can more effectively illustrate and demonstrate specific selling concepts. The use of realistic exercises aids the student in taking the subject matter beyond imaginary applications. As a result, the students' understanding of and ability to apply selling concepts are greatly advanced. In turn, the students' self-confidence is enhanced through their many positive accomplishments. Students working with experiential exercises as supplements to textbooks and lectures indicate that classes become more interesting and exciting—learning can be fun. As a result of increased student involvement, attention spans are amplified and increasingly focused toward the selling concepts being studied.

The Professional Selling Skills Workbook, includes a strong selection of exercises emphasizing the relational aspects of consultative, needs-satisfaction selling. Gathered from colleagues at colleges, universities, and corporate training centers across the country, each exercise was originally developed and written by experienced sales educators and practitioners. Each exercise offers the additional benefit of having already been pretested and proven in the classroom. In fact, the exercises presented in this edition are the result of several years of development, testing, and revision by educators and students at several universities and colleges.

Each exercise is presented in a consistently "user-friendly" format that includes a description of specific learning objectives, an introductory discussion, and a clear and complete specification of the exercise assignment. Cognitive questions are included within exercises for the purpose of coaching and facilitating class discussion following class activities. Where applicable, pre-printed worksheets are provided for students to use in completing exercise assignments. Each worksheet page is perforated along the bound edge to facilitate turning work in for evaluation and credit.

The requirement for turning in completed work on a regular basis (that is, daily or weekly) serves as a positive reinforcement in two important areas. First, it provides a quick and efficient method for the instructor to evaluate the progress of individual students and the class as a whole. The common format provided by the pre-printed worksheets offers students a guideline for developing and organizing their thoughts and responses. A second benefit comes in the fact that regular assignments, both in and out of class, assist participants in keeping up with reading and study assignments.

Reflecting the depth and variety of activities included, the book offers 68 exercises illustrating and demonstrating each of the principles and concepts fundamental to professional selling. As such, this book is an excellent supplement that is easily adapted to any selling textbook that might be used in the course. While many exercises are designed to complement each other, each exercise is fully self-supporting. No exercise depends on a previous exercise or acts as required background for any upcoming exercise. This allows maximum flexibility in tailoring the exercises to fit any presentation order.

For convenience and clarity, exercises are grouped by subject categories. A review of the subject categories listed below will evidence the current nature of each of the exercises and the significant inclusion of communication skills and relationship building behaviors in addition to the more traditional exercises built around the selling process itself.

Module 1	Discovering Personal Selling as a Career
Module 2	Trust-Based Relationship Selling
Module 3	The Trust-Based Relationship Selling Process
Module 4	Understanding Buyer Expectations and Behavior
Module 5	Communication Skills
Module 6	Questioning Skills
Module 7	Listening Skills
Module 8	Written Communication Skills
Module 9	Strategic Prospecting Skills
Module 10	Sales Presentation Skills
Module 11	Skills for Earning Commitment and Negotiating Resistance
Module 12	Skills for Developing and Enhancing Buyer–Seller Relationships

ACKNOWLEDGMENTS

The Professiona Selling Skills Workbook has benefitted from the advice and contributions of many colleagues and friends, In particular, we would like to thank Lyn Hastert Maize, Paul Stewart, Jim Lizotte, and especially Jim Patterson for their assistance in the formation of this book. We would especially like to thank the following colleagues who contributed experiential exercises to be included in the workbook:

Jill S. Attaway
    Department of Marketing, Illinois State University

Brett A. Boyle
    Department of Marketing, DePaul University

Joseph A. Chapman
    Department of Marketing, Ball State University

Dan T. Dunn, Jr.
    Department of Marketing, Northeastern University

Michael A. Humphreys
    Department of Marketing, Illinois State University

Patricia A. Knowles
    Department of Marketing, Clemson University

Timothy A. Longfellow
    Department of Marketing, Illinois State University

Mike R. Luthy
    College of Business, Drake University

Greg W. Marshall
    Department of Marketing, University of South Florida

Donald A. McBane
    Department of Marketing, Clemson University

Robin T. Peterson
    Department of Marketing, New Mexico State University

Norris E. Porter
    Academic Advising, Illinois State University

Gary Rhoads
    Department of Marketing, Brigham Young University

Camille P. Schuster
   Department of Marketing, Xavier University

Sue Stewart-Belle
   Department of Management, Illinois State University

In addition, the following reviewers gave of their time and insight to improve the manuscript in its many stages.

Jill S. Attaway
   Department of Marketing, Illinois State University

Joseph A. Chapman
   Department of Marketing, Ball State University

Jon Hawes
   Department of Marketing, University of Akron

Michael A. Humphreys
   Department of Marketing, Illinois State University

William L. Kindsfather
   Business Department, Tarrant County Junior College

Timothy A. Longfellow
   Department of Marketing, Illinois State University

Don Shemwell
   Department of Marketing, East Tennessee State University

Sue Stewart-Belle
   Department of Management, Illinois State University

This workbook has been carefully developed to function as an integral part of your professional selling learning experience. The wide variety of experiential exercises and cognitive discussion questions are based on actual selling situations. As a result they should be very beneficial as you learn and enhance your selling skills. As you use the workbook, you may have ideas regarding how the workload could be improved to further assist students such as yourself. We sincerely welcome any of your ideas and comments. Good luck and best wishes for an exciting and successful career in professional selling.

Ramon A. Avila
Ball State University

Thomas N. Ingram
Colorado State University

Raymond W. LaForge
University of Louisville

Michael R. Williams
Illinois State University

November 1995

CONTENTS

THE PROFESSIONAL SELLING SKILLS
WORKBOOK

MODULE ONE

DISCOVERING PROFESSIONAL SELLING AS A CAREER

Professional selling, at first glance, is probably most often thought of as a business activity. A more realistic examination of professional selling, its objectives as well as its activities, would reveal that professional selling is actually a much more generalized activity occurring across virtually all settings and situations—business and non-business alike. In fact we are all salespeople. The ability to work with others to inform, persuade, and develop mutually beneficial relationships is critical to all of us. Consequently, understanding and successfully practicing these skills of professional selling should be important to everyone regardless of their job title or role in life.

Within the business environment the image and role of the professional salesperson continues to evolve. The emergence of relationship marketing as a fundamental operating philosophy necessary for success in today's fragmented and highly competitive marketplace, has enhanced and placed renewed emphasis on the important role played by salespeople. Salespeople have the most direct contact with customers, and buyers often perceive the conduct and behavior of the salesperson as personifying how the selling firm feels about its customers. Recognizing that the very success of a firm's relationship marketing strategies is highly dependent upon its sales representatives has brought about major changes in the activities and process of selling and magnified the benefits of professional selling as a career.

Taking on the expanded roles of business consultant and relationship manager, the salesperson serves as a strategic problem solver and source of unique added-value product components. Reflecting the vital link salespeople provide between a company and its customers, perceptions and attitudes toward professional selling are changing. As a result of these changes, professional selling is evolving as a meaningful business activity. Experiential Exercise 1.1 (*Discovering Attitudes Toward Sales Careers*) addresses these changing perceptions and attitudes. By completing this self-assessment survey instrument, you can better understand your own personal perceptions, discuss them, and compare them with those of other class members.

Harcourt Brace & Company

While professional selling positions still serve as beginning points of employment in many organizations, the many personal benefits and rewards accruing through active and professional selling responsibilities result in a high number of salespeople electing to remain in professional selling as a career. As a result, more and more organizations are actively increasing the variety of optional career opportunities available through the selling track. Experiential Exercise 1.2 (*What Are the Options?*) is designed to assist you in exploring the many sales career options available. In addition to immersing you into the various types of selling careers, Exercise 1.2 assists you in putting together a list of specific industries and organizations to target in your job search.

Transitioning from the broader issues of professional selling as a career, Exercises 1.3 (*Words Which Identify Salespeople and a Sales Career*), 1.4 (*How Salespeople Spend Their Time*), and 1.5 (*What Attributes Are Essential to a Successful Sales Career?*) provide a more micro focus into the activities of a salesperson. Exercise 1.3 activates the descriptive words and phrases commonly associated with personal selling. Integrating your thoughts with other class members in an open class discussion offers the foundation for enriching your knowledge of the role and activities performed by salespeople. Exercise 1.4 continues to build on your understanding of "just what does a salesperson do" by examining how the salesperson must split available time among selling activities, travel and waiting time, performing various administrative tasks, attending meetings, and nurturing customer relationships by following-up-sales and servicing new and prospective accounts. Many individuals are surprised to learn that typical salespeople spend less than one-half of their available time in actual selling activities.

Building on your understanding of the role and activities performed by a salesperson, Experiential Exercise 1.5 returns to the age old question, "Are salespeople made or born?" Many stereotypes exist regarding the profile of a successful salesperson. However, as a reflection of the diverse roles played by salespeople across different industries, companies, customers, and selling situations, it is doubtful that any single listing of attributes could sufficiently profile the successful salesperson. Some of the more commonly listed attributes for success in selling include: outgoing, enthusiastic, motivated, ethical, responsible, self-confident, competitive, and persistent. Observing that these success traits would probably hold true for any occupation, Ingram and LaForge (1992) synthesize several major studies investigating this topic and provide the following list of five factors that appear to be critical to selling:[1]

EMPATHY	the ability to see things as others would see them
EGO DRIVE	the degree of determination that an individual has to achieve goals and overcome obstacles in striving for success
EGO STRENGTH	the degree to which an individual is self-assured and self-accepting

---

[1]Ingram, T. N. and R. W. LaForge, *Sales Management: Analysis and Decision Making* (Fort Worth, TX, The Dryden Press, 1992).

VERBAL COMMUNICATION SKILLS	the skill an individual possesses in effective listening and questioning
ENTHUSIASM	a general zest for life's everyday occurrences and a genuine passion for personal selling

Each of the experiential exercises in this first module is designed to help you: think through and better understand the importance of professional selling; understand the various options offered through professional selling as a career; and finally, learn what it takes to be a successful salesperson. Understanding your personal perceptions and attitudes toward professional selling, possible career options offered, and personal attributes required can provide valuable assistance in making your job choice.

DISCOVERING PROFESSIONAL SELLING AS A CAREER
EXPERIENTIAL EXERCISE 1.1
Discovering Attitudes Toward Sales Careers

OBJECTIVE: You will evaluate and understand your own attitudes toward professional selling as a career and develop a sense of how and why this attitude varies from individual to individual.

THE EXERCISE ASSIGNMENT

Please complete the following survey by circling the number corresponding to your degree of agreement or disagreement for each of the statements. The meaning of the numbers is as follows:

1 Strongly Disagree
2 Disagree
3 Neither Agree or Disagree
4 Agree
5 Strongly Agree

I ASSOCIATE A JOB IN PROFESSIONAL SELLING WITH:	STRONGLY DISAGREE				STRONGLY AGREE
Frustration	1	2	3	4	5
Insincerity and deceit	1	2	3	4	5
Low status/low prestige	1	2	3	4	5
Much traveling	1	2	3	4	5
Salespeople being "money hungry"	1	2	3	4	5
High pressure; forcing people to buy unwanted goods	1	2	3	4	5
Low job security	1	2	3	4	5
"Just a job," not a "career"	1	2	3	4	5
Uninteresting/no challenge	1	2	3	4	5
No need for creativity	1	2	3	4	5
Personality is crucial	1	2	3	4	5
Too little monetary reward	1	2	3	4	5
Interferes with home life	1	2	3	4	5
I prefer a nonsales position much more than a sales position	1	2	3	4	5

Harcourt Brace & Company

SCORING YOUR SURVEY

When you have complete the survey by circling a number for each and every item, **add** each of the numbers you circled and enter the **sum** here: _____

Now, **divide** the sum on the line above by 14, and enter the answer: _____

This final number (it should be a number between 1 and 5) represents your overall attitude toward sales as a career, based on these 14 attributes. A score below 3 (disagreement with the statement) would indicate a positive attitude toward sales, while a score above 3 (agreement with the statement) would signify a negative attitude toward sales as a career.

Experience indicates that comparing the results from this survey typically leads to a lively discussion. By all means—do join in!! Among many others, some specific items you might want to examine and discuss are:

1. How does your overall score compare with those of others in the class?

   _____

   Can you identify any possible reasons these differences exist? _____

   _____

   _____

   _____

2. Are your scores for any specific items significantly different (that is, more positive/negative toward sales as a career) from the scores for other statements on your survey?

   _____

   _____

   _____

   Can you identify any possible reasons for these differences? _____

   _____

   _____

Harcourt Brace & Company

DISCOVERING PROFESSIONAL SELLING AS A CAREER
EXPERIENTIAL EXERCISE 1.2
What Are the Options?

OBJECTIVE: You will narrow down sales career options. This exercise provides you with a framework for and experience in setting up your "focus set" of firms in which to explore job possibilities and opportunities.

WHAT TYPE OF SELLING DO YOU PREFER?

As your first step toward identifying companies that you might like to work for, you need to make a basic decision as to what type of selling activities you prefer. There are a multitude of career options available in selling. As the role of the professional salesperson continues to evolve and organizations actively increase the career opportunities available through the selling track, the term salesperson loses more and more meaning as a unique descriptor. Offering a framework for examining the diverse selling career options available, Ingram and LaForge (1992)[1] identify and discuss six basic classifications of selling: Sales Support, New Business Sales, Existing Business Sales, Inside Sales, Direct-to-Consumer Sales, and Combination Sales Jobs.

Sales Support. Sales support personnel are typically not directly involved in the actual selling process. Instead, they fulfill the role of disseminating information and performing other activities designed to stimulate and support sales. Often part of a selling team, support salespeople may report to a salesperson, who has responsibility for the overall selling process, or to a sales manager. Two well-known categories of sales support personnel are (a) missionary or detail salespeople and (b) technical support salespeople. Missionary salespeople are customary in the grocery industry with detail salespeople commonly found in the pharmaceutical industry. Technical support salespeople assist in design, installation, training, and follow-up services of a technical nature.

New Business Sales. Working to develop new customers and introduce new customers to the marketplace, new business salespeople are at the heart of an organization's sales growth objectives. The two primary classifications of new business salespeople are (a) pioneers and (b) order-getters. Pioneers are involved with new products and new customers. Order-getters work in highly competitive environments seeking to sell existing customers new or additional items in the product line. The pressure to perform is fairly intense in both forms

Harcourt Brace & Company

[1]Ingram, T. N. and R. W. LaForge, *Sales Management: Analysis and Decision Making* (Fort Worth, TX, The Dryden Press, 1992).

of new business selling. These selling roles require insight, creative selling, and the ability to effectively work through the resistance to change which is common with prospective customers.

Existing Business Sales. Many organizations are finding that it is easier to protect and retain existing customers than it is to find and develop replacement customers. Maintaining relationships with existing customers is the primary role of existing business salespeople. These salespeople are just as valuable to an organization as new business salespeople, however, insightful and creative selling skills are less important for this category of salesperson. Rather, their strengths tend to be in the areas of reliability, competence, and ability to provide the customer with assurance.

Inside Sales. Inside salespeople refers to non-retail salespeople who work with customers inside the organization's place of business. Inside sales can be classified as either active or passive in nature. Active inside sales includes involvement in the complete selling process, possibly as part of a telemarketing strategy or when customers come to the place of business for the purpose of buying. Passive inside selling involves the acceptance, rather than the solicitation, of customer orders. Inside sales has received considerable attention as a supplement, and even alternative, to traditional field selling.

Direct-to Consumer Sales. There are 4 million retail salespeople and perhaps another million selling real estate, insurance, and financial services. There are more salespeople in this diverse group than in any other classification. Salespeople active in this form of selling include the part-time, and often temporary, salesperson in a retail store as well as highly trained and professional stockbrokers.

Combination Sales Jobs. It is not uncommon to find selling positions that include some combination of the preceding 5 types of selling. For instance, many salespeople are given responsibility for managing a territory. Within their territory, these salespeople are responsible for maintaining (existing business) and further developing (order-getters) existing customers, identifying and selling new prospects (pioneer), and providing follow-up information and services (sales support). It is also common to find salespeople having responsibilities for both field sales and inside sales. An example would be salespeople who travel their territories calling on existing customers (existing business) and prospects (new business) several days a week, but who also have telemarketing responsibilities (inside sales) one or two days during the week.

THE EXERCISE ASSIGNMENT

Using the preceding six basic classifications of selling as a guide, **circle the column heading** in the following table that corresponds to the type of selling activity you prefer. Next, consider the different industries (far left column) that might be open to you within that specific type of selling. As you consider the possible industries that are attractive to you, rank your five most preferred choices by placing the corresponding ranking number in the proper cell of the column (1 indicating your top choice and 5 indicating your fifth choice).

Harcourt Brace & Company

Considering your choices, use your own base of experience, input from other knowledgeable people (parents, relatives, friends and acquaintances, faculty, and library/career placement resources) to identify ten companies that are active in each of the five cells that you have chosen on the matrix. These 50 companies should become your "career focus companies"—companies on which you are going to place a priority focus for your job search. Now that you have identified your priority companies, you should (a) learn all you can about each of them, (b) identify an effective point of contact that can get you into the companies' recruiting processes, and (c) make the necessary contacts to get your cover letter and resume placed for consideration.

Harcourt Brace & Company

INDUSTRY CLASSIFICATION	SALES SUPPORT	NEW-BUSINESS SALES	EXISTING SALES	INSIDE SALES	DIRECT-TO-CONSUMER SALES	COMBINATION SALES JOBS
Business Services						
Communications						
Electronics						
Fabricated Metals						
Health Services						
Drugs						
Insurance						
Machinery						
Manufacturing						
Paper and Allied Products						
Printing/Publishing						
Hotels/Lodging						
Other						
Other						
Other						
Other						
Other						
Other						
Other						

Harcourt Brace & Company

DISCOVERING PROFESSIONAL SELLING AS A CAREER
EXPERIENTIAL EXERCISE 1.3
Words Which Identify Salespeople and a Sales Career

OBJECTIVE: You will be able to express how you feel about salespeople and a sales career.

THE EXERCISE ASSIGNMENT

What words can you think of that describe a salesperson?

1. _____ Why? _____

   _____

2. _____ Why? _____

   _____

3. _____ Why? _____

   _____

4. _____ Why? _____

   _____

5. _____ Why? _____

   _____

6. _____ Why? _____

   _____

7. _____ Why? _____

   _____

Harcourt Brace & Company

Were your words generally positive? _____ Yes _____ No

Why? _____

_____

_____

Were your words generally negative? _____ Yes _____ No

Why? _____

_____

_____

What words can you think of that describe a sales career?

1. _____ Why? _____

_____

_____

2. _____ Why? _____

_____

_____

3. _____ Why? _____

_____

_____

4. _____ Why? _____

_____

_____

5. _____ Why? _____

_____

_____

Harcourt Brace & Company

6. _____ Why? _____

_____

_____

7. _____ Why? _____

_____

_____

Were your words generally positive? _____ Yes _____ No

Why? _____

_____

_____

Were your words generally negative? _____ Yes _____ No

Why? _____

_____

_____

◉

DISCOVERING PROFESSIONAL SELLING AS A CAREER
EXPERIENTIAL EXERCISE 1.4
How Salespeople Spend Their Time

✳

OBJECTIVE: You will be able to determine the scope of a salesperson's job and how salespeople spend their time.

THE EXERCISE ASSIGNMENT

Based on your knowledge of a sales career, how do you think a salesperson spends his or her time? What sales activities will a typical salesperson be responsible for?

1. Activity: _____

    _____

2. Activity: _____

    _____

3. Activity: _____

    _____

4. Activity: _____

    _____

5. Activity: _____

    _____

6. Activity: _____

    _____

7. Activity: _____

    _____

Harcourt Brace & Company

8. Activity: _____

_____

9. Activity: _____

_____

10. Activity: _____

_____

11. Activity: _____

_____

12. Activity: _____

_____

13. Activity: _____

_____

14. Activity: _____

_____

15. Activity: _____

_____

Harcourt Brace & Company

DISCOVERING PROFESSIONAL SELLING AS A CAREER
EXPERIENTIAL EXERCISE 1.5
What Attributes Are Essential to a Successful Sales Career?

OBJECTIVE: You will be able to determine what characteristics are essential for a successful salesperson.

THE EXERCISE ASSIGNMENT

Based on your knowledge of salespeople you have been around, what characteristics do you believe are essential for success in selling? Why?

1. Characteristic _____ Why? _____

   _____

   _____

2. Characteristic _____ Why? _____

   _____

   _____

3. Characteristic _____ Why? _____

   _____

   _____

4. Characteristic _____ Why? _____

   _____

   _____

5. Characteristic _____   Why? _____

_____

_____

6. Characteristic _____   Why? _____

_____

_____

7. Characteristic _____   Why? _____

_____

_____

8. Characteristic _____   Why? _____

_____

_____

9. Characteristic _____   Why? _____

_____

_____

10. Characteristic _____   Why? _____

_____

_____

11. Characteristic _____   Why? _____

_____

_____

12. Characteristic _____   Why? _____

_____

_____

Harcourt Brace & Company

MODULE TWO

TRUST-BASED RELATIONSHIP SELLING

Reflecting the complexity of today's intensely competitive and fast changing business environment, buyers are requiring continuous increases in quality along with higher levels of service. Buying organizations continue making cuts in the number of suppliers, preferring to work very closely with a reduced set of firms as a means to lower both product and acquisition costs, while simultaneously maximizing quality and performance. These preferred outcomes are based on developing relationships between the buyer and seller that encourage the mutual sharing of information and collaborative problem solving. Characterized by win-win outcomes facilitating the fulfillment of goals for all parties involved, these alliances tend to be long-term in nature and demand high levels of mutual trust in order to be successful.

The emergence of this trust-based, relationship selling paradigm carries significant implications for the roles played by salespeople. The transactional focus of traditional selling practices are no longer sufficient for success in the new business environment. Based on an adversarial, win-lose model of negotiation, many of the salesperson's transaction-focused roles and activities actually counter the development of trust. On the other hand, relationship selling requires the salesperson to take on a strategic role of business consultant and long-term ally who is highly involved as a trusted, key player in the customer's business. The following table[1] illustrates the implications for a salesperson through a comparison of transaction-focused and trust-based relationship selling:

[1]Adapted from Corcoran, K. J., L. K. Peterson, D. B. Baitch, M. F. Barrett, *High Performace Sales Organizations: Creating Competitive Advantage in the Global Marketplace* (Chicago: Irwin Professional Publishing, 1995).

Harcourt Brace & Company

A COMPARISON OF TRANSACTION-FOCUSED TRADITIONAL SELLING WITH TRUST-BASED RELATIONSHIP SELLING

	TRANSACTION-FOCUSED TRADITIONAL SELLING	TRUST-BASED RELATIONSHIP SELLING
PRIMARY PERSPECTIVE	The Salesperson and Selling Firm	The Customer and the Customer's Customers
DESIRED OUTCOME	Closed Sales, Order Volume	Trust, Joint Planning, Mutual Benefits, Enhance Profits
ROLE OF SALESPERSON	Make Calls and Close Sales	Business Consultant and Long-Term Ally Key Player in the Customer's Business
NATURE OF COMMUNICATION	One-way, from Salesperson to Customer	Two-Way and Collaborative
DEGREE OF SALESPERSON'S INVOLVEMENT IN CUSTOMER'S DECISION MAKING PROCESS	Isolated from Customer's Decision Making Process	Actively Involved in Customer's Decision Making Process
KNOWLEDGE REQUIRED	Own Company's Products Competition Applications Account Strategies Costs Opportunities	Own Company's Products and Resources Competition Applications Account Strategies Costs Opportunities General Business and Industry Knowledge and Insight Customer's Products, Competition, and Customers
TYPICAL SKILLS REQUIRED	Selling Skills	Selling Skills Information Gathering Listening and Questioning Strategic Problem Solving Creating and Demonstrating Unique, Value-Added Solutions Teambuilding and Teamwork
POST SALE FOLLOW-UP	Little or None: Move on to Conquer Next Customer	Continued Follow-Through to: Assure Customer Satisfaction Keep Customer Informed Add Customer-Value Manage Opportunities

Harcourt Brace & Company

Integral to the relationship selling paradigm, five types of selling behaviors are supported as being positively associated with the trust between buyer and seller that are crucial for initiating, developing, and enhancing productive relationships.[2] These types of behavior are summarized below:

CUSTOMER-ORIENTATION

- You understand the buyer's needs and place them on par with your own (and your organization's).
- You give fair and balanced presentations (pros and cons) and clear statements of benefits.
- You advise rather than "sell" (you won't push a product the buyer doesn't need).

COMPETENCE

- You display technical command of products and applications (that is, you are accurate, complete, and objective).
- You have the skill, knowledge, time, and resources to do what you promise and what the buyer wants.
- Your words and actions are consistent with a professional image.

DEPENDABILITY

- Your actions fulfill your prior promises.
- Your actions fit a pattern of prior dependable actions you have established.
- You refuse to promise what you can't deliver.

CANDOR

- Your presentations are balanced and fair (for example, product limitations as well as advantages and benefits are discussed).
- What you say agrees with what the buyer knows to be true.
- The proof you use to support your words is credible.
- Subsequent events prove your statements to be true.

LIKABILITY

- You make efficient use of the buyer's time.
- You are courteous and polite.
- You and the buyer share and talk about areas of commonality, including goals and interests. This also extends to non-business topics.

As discussed above, relationship selling emphasizes a very different set of skills and attitudes than those commonly found in transaction-focused selling. Relationship selling requires a salesperson to establish and demonstrate trustworthiness. High pressure selling

Harcourt Brace & Company

---

[2] Adapted from Doyle, S. X. and G. T. Roth, "Selling and Sales Management in Action: The Use of Insight and Coaching to Improve Relationship Selling," *Journal of Personal Selling and Sales Management,* Winter 1992, p. 62; in Ingram, T. N., *Certification Study Guide,* The University of Memphis: SMEI Accreditation Institute, 1994.

methods based on "*closing early and closing often*" are taboo in relationship selling. The exercises in this module are designed to enhance your understanding of these differences and your ablility to practice trust-based relationship selling.

Experiential Exercises 2.1 (*Scenario for Trust Building*) places you into an actual selling situation and requires you to apply the five trust builders discussed above in resolving certain problems that have developed. Exercise 2.2 (*Building Buyer's Trust*) further builds on your understanding of trust building behaviors by translating the five trust builders into actual actions that you might undertake as a salesperson. Exercise 2.3 (*Assessing Sales Ethics*) illustrates that behaviors considered to be professional and even legal are not necessarily ethical. Exercise 2.4 (*Ethics Scale*) surveys your personal perspective on the ethics of a variety of situations common to personal selling. These self-assessment instruments have been used for several years in industry and provide a rich and interesting subject for class discussion and comparison. Exercise 2.5 (*Salesperson and Buyer Interviews*) brings a touch of reality into your relationship selling experience by going into the field to observe and/or interview a salesperson and a buyer. These interviews focus on activities and expectations associated with relationship selling. Further extending your understanding of relationship selling and interaction with actual salespeople, Experiential Exercise 2.6 (*Assessing the Lifetime Value of a Customer*) involves your shadowing—accompanying and observing—a salesperson as calls are made. In collaboration with your chosen salesperson, the lifetime value of an actual customer is computed and "real-time" relationship selling activities are observed and discussed.

TRUST-BASED RELATIONSHIP SELLING
EXPERIENTIAL EXERCISE 2.1
Scenario for Trust Building

OBJECTIVE: You will understand the concept of trust-based relationship selling, and why it is preferred by both customers and sales professionals. You will identify attributes that enable salespeople to build trust and the implications of those attributes for salespeople in working with their customers.

THE EXERCISE ASSIGNMENT

Relationship selling is directed toward achieving mutually satisfying results between buyer and seller that sustain and enhance future interactions. In the past several years, there has been a growing recognition that adversarial, "me against you" buyer–seller relationships are often nonproductive for both parties. The director of Xerox's training university in Leesburg, Virginia, says the biggest change in its sales training in the past decade is that "we spend a lot more time on what the customer thinks is important."

Competition has intensified, technology has advanced, and pressure to improve productivity has soared. Given these changes in the marketplace, many firms are cutting down on the number of approved vendors. People are busier than ever, and there is no time for the misinformation and posturing often associated with the old style of selling. In a nutshell, it's increasingly productive to work closely with customers.

Relationship selling requires a different set of skills and attitudes than is true for transaction-oriented selling. Questioning and listening become more important than talking. High-pressure sales approaches and gimmicky closing methods are taboo in relationship selling. Personality matters, but not as much as appealing to the buyer's rational side in an interesting, well-illustrated, concise manner.

Trust-Building Sales Behavior

To initiate, develop, and enhance customer relationships, salespeople must demonstrate their trustworthiness. As detailed in the introduction to this module, research has identified five characteristics of trust-building salespeople:

1. **Customer Orientation**—Placing as much emphasis on the customer's interest as your own.

2. **Competence**—The ability, knowledge, and resources to meet customer expectations.

Harcourt Brace & Company

3. **Dependability**—The predictability of your actions.

4. **Candor**—Honesty of the spoken word.

5. **Likability**—Rooted in each party's perception of "having something in common" with the other. Admittedly an emotional factor, difficult to pin down, yet a powerful force in some buyer–seller relationships.

What are your ideas about how you can improve your trust-building behavior as you interact with customers?

IDEAS FOR ACTION

CUSTOMER ORIENTATION

_____

_____

_____

_____

_____

COMPETENCE

_____

_____

_____

_____

_____

DEPENDABILITY

_____

_____

_____

_____

CANDOR

_____

_____

_____

_____

LIKABILITY

_____

_____

_____

_____

_____

◉

TRUST-BASED RELATIONSHIP SELLING
EXPERIENTIAL EXERCISE 2.2
Building Buyer's Trust

OBJECTIVE: You will understand how specific salesperson behaviors generate buyer's trust and you will be able to apply the five trust-building behaviors.

THE EXERCISE ASSIGNMENT

Congratulations! As a new salesperson for Schmidt Business Forms, you have just completed training and have been assigned the Southwest territory. Schmidt Business Forms designs and manufactures a full line of both stock and customized forms for use in all types of business. Operating throughout the United States and Canada, Schmidt is reconigized as one of the three leaders in the industry.

Doctors' General Hospital was once a major account in your territory. Nevertheless, over this past year virtually all the hospital's forms business has been switched from Schmidt to one of your main competitors. Due to the large volume and many types of forms used, Doctors' has placed the purchasing responsibility for all forms in the hands of Jim Adams in the Purchasing Department. An experienced professional purchasing agent, Jim has been in this position for several years and has purchased significant volumes of forms from Schmidt in the past. In the course of calling on Jim at his office in the hospital, you have learned that Doctors' dropping Schmidt as a forms source did not happen overnight. Although the loss of this account was not related to any one single problem, you have learned that the switch to your competitor was basically due to a combination of events that resulted in a loss of trust in Schmidt. Several shipments did not arrive as promised, causing major problems for both billing and admissions. Even though the final proof copies were correct, a newly designed, multipart computer form was found to be short one of its pages. This required emergency room staff to take time and use a copier (located one floor up) until the forms could be rerun and delivered two weeks later. The final straw concerned an admissions form that Schmidt had been supplying the hospital for over three years. For some reason, a new shipment of the admissions forms was the wrong size and would not fit into patient files without being folded. In each event, the prior salesperson worked with Jim Adams to get the problems resolved and the correct forms delivered. Discounts were also given to help offset the inconvenience incurred. Nevertheless, Schmidt has lost the account, the previous salesperson has quit the company, and you have inherited the challenge of winning back Jim Adams and Doctors' Hospital.

Put yourself in the role of the salesperson for Schmidt Business Forms in the selling situation just described and review the five *Trust-Building Behaviors* presented in the

Harcourt Brace & Company

preceding introduction to this module. Using the following worksheet as a guide, discuss and give examples of how you might utilize each of the five *Trust-Builders* to re-establish a relationship with Jim Adams and win back the Doctors' Hospital account.

Trust-Building Worksheet

1. Customer Orientation (Intent):

   _____

   _____

   _____

   _____

   _____

   _____

   _____

   _____

   _____

2. Competence (Ability):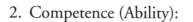

   _____

   _____

   _____

   _____

   _____

   _____

Harcourt Brace & Company

_____

_____

_____

3. Dependability (Actions):

_____

_____

_____

_____

_____

_____

_____

4. Candor (Words):

_____

_____

_____

_____

_____

_____

_____

_____

_____

_____

5. Likability:

_____

_____

_____

_____

_____

_____

_____

_____

◉

TRUST-BASED RELATIONSHIP SELLING
EXPERIENTIAL EXERCISE 2.3
Assessing Sales Ethics

✳

OBJECTIVES: You will understand that there is a fine line between what is ethical and what is not ethical.

THE EXERCISE ASSIGNMENT

Sales professionalism requires a truthful, customer-oriented approach. Customers are increasingly intolerant of nonprofessional, unethical sales practices. Assess the following statements as to their legality, ethicalness, and professionalism.

Please circle your response for each category.

1. Salesperson shows concern for his or her own interests, not that of the client.

   legal/illegal   ethical/unethical   professional/unprofessional

2. Pass the blame for something he or she did wrong.

   legal/illegal   ethical/unethical   professional/unprofessional

3. Take advantage of the poor or uneducated.

   legal/illegal   ethical/unethical   professional/unprofessional

4. Accept favors from customers so the seller feels obliged to bend policies.

   legal/illegal   ethical/unethical   professional/unprofessional

5. Sell products or services that people do not need.

   legal/illegal   ethical/unethical   professional/unprofessional

6. Give answers when he or she does not really know answers.

   legal/illegal   ethical/unethical   professional/unprofessional

Harcourt Brace & Company

7. Pose as market researcher when doing phone sales.

   legal/illegal   **ethical/unethical**   **professional/unprofessional**

8. Sell dangerous or hazardous products.

   legal/illegal   **ethical/unethical**   **professional/unprofessional**

9. Withhold information.

   legal/illegal   **ethical/unethical**   **professional/unprofessional**

10. Exaggerate benefits of product.

    legal/illegal   **ethical/unethical**   **professional/unprofessional**

11. Lie about availability of product in order to make sale.

    legal/illegal   **ethical/unethical**   **professional/unprofessional**

12. Lie to competitors.

    legal/illegal   **ethical/unethical**   **professional/unprofessional**

13. Falsify product testimonials.

    legal/illegal   **ethical/unethical**   **professional/unprofessional**

Source: Adapted from Trawick, I. F., J. E. Swan, G. W. McGee, and D. R. Rink, *Journal of The Academy of Marketing Science,* 1991, Vol. 19, No. 1, p. 17–23; Dubinsky, A. J. and T. N. Ingram, "Correlates of Salespeople Ethical Conflict: An Exploratory Investigation," *Journal of Business Ethics,* 3, 1984, p. 343–353; Dubinsky, A. J. and I. M. Gwin, "Business Ethics: Buyers and Sellers," *Journal of Purchasing and Materials Management,* Winter 1981, Vol. 17, p. 9–16.

Harcourt Brace & Company

TRUST-BASED RELATIONSHIP SELLING
EXPERIENTIAL EXERCISE 2.4
Ethics Scale

OBJECTIVE: You will develop an understanding of the multitude of ethical situations that exist.

THE EXERCISE ASSIGNMENT

How ethical is each of the following situations? Be prepared to defend your answer. Please circle your response for each situation.

1. The salesperson seeks confidential information about competitors by questioning suppliers.

    very ethical   ethical   neither   unethical   very unethical

2. The salesperson seeks information from the purchaser on competitors' quotations for the purpose of submitting another quotation.

    very ethical   ethical   neither   unethical   very unethical

3. The buyer gives the salesperson information on competitors' quotations, then allows him or her to requote.

    very ethical   ethical   neither   unethical   very unethical

4. The buyer exaggerates the seriousness of a problem to a salesperson in order to get a better price or some other concession.

    very ethical   ethical   neither   unethical   very unethical

5. To obtain a lower price or other concession, the buyer *falsely* informs an existing supplier that the company may use another source.

    very ethical   ethical   neither   unethical   very unethical

Harcourt Brace & Company

6. The buyer solicits quotations from new sources, when a marked preference for existing suppliers is the norm, merely to fill a quota for bids.

    very ethical   **ethical**   **neither**   **unethical**   **very unethical**

7. The salesperson attempts to get the buyer to divulge competitors' bids in low-bid buying situations.

    very ethical   **ethical**   **neither**   **unethical**   **very unethical**

8. The salesperson exaggerates how quickly orders will be delivered to get a sale.

    very ethical   **ethical**   **neither**   **unethical**   **very unethical**

9. The salesperson lets it be known that he or she has information about a competitor if purchasing agent is interested.

    very ethical   **ethical**   **neither**   **unethical**   **very unethical**

10. The salesperson hints that, if order is placed, the price might be lower on the next order, when it is not so.

    very ethical   **ethical**   **neither**   **unethical**   **very unethical**

11. The salesperson stresses only positive aspects of the product, omitting possible problems the purchasing firm might have with it.

    very ethical   **ethical**   **neither**   **unethical**   **very unethical**

12. The buyer allows such factors as race, sex, ethnic group affiliation, and religious persuasion to affect salesperson selection.

    very ethical   **ethical**   **neither**   **unethical**   **very unethical**

13. The buyer discriminates against a vendor whose salespeople use "back-door" selling instead of going through purchasing department.

    very ethical   **ethical**   **neither**   **unethical**   **very unethical**

14. The buyer discriminates on the basis of nepotism. (Nepotism is used here in a broad sense to cover all preferential treatment extended to suppliers who are relatives or friends, or are recommended by higher management.)

    very ethical   **ethical**   **neither**   **unethical**   **very unethical**

Harcourt Brace & Company

15. In a shortage situation, the salesperson allocates product shipments to purchasing agents the seller personally likes.

   very ethical   **ethical**   **neither**   **unethical**   **very unethical**

16. In order to obtain a lower price or other concession, the buyer informs an existing supplier that the company may use a second source.

   very ethical   **ethical**   **neither**   **unethical**   **very unethical**

17. In a reciprocal buying situation, salesperson hints that unless an order is forthcoming, the prospect's sales to the selling firm might suffer.

   very ethical   **ethical**   **neither**   **unethical**   **very unethical**

18. The salesperson attempts to use the economic power of the firm to obtain concessions from the buyer.

   very ethical   **ethical**   **neither**   **unethical**   **very unethical**

19. The salesperson has less competitive prices or other terms for buyers who depend on the firm as the sole source of supply.

   very ethical   **ethical**   **neither**   **unethical**   **very unethical**

20. The buyer accepts from a supplier gifts such as sales promotion prizes and "purchase volume incentives."

   very ethical   **ethical**   **neither**   **unethical**   **very unethical**

21. The buyer accepts trips, meals, or other free entertainment.

   very ethical   **ethical**   **neither**   **unethical**   **very unethical**

22. The salesperson gives a purchaser who was one of the best customers a gift worth $50 or more at Christmas or other occasions.

   very ethical   **ethical**   **neither**   **unethical**   **very unethical**

23. The salesperson gives a potential customer a gift worth $50 or more at Christmas or other occasions.

   very ethical   **ethical**   **neither**   **unethical**   **very unethical**

Harcourt Brace & Company

24. The salesperson grants price concessions to purchasing agents of companies in which the salesperson owns stock.

   very ethical   ethical   neither   unethical   very unethical

25. The salesperson attempts to sell to a purchasing agent a product that has little or no value to buyer's company.

   very ethical   ethical   neither   unethical   very unethical

Source: Adapted from Trawick, I. F., J. E. Swan, G. W. McGee, and D. R. Rink, *Journal of The Academy of Marketing Science,* 1991, Vol. 19, No. 1, p. 17–23; Dubinsky, A. J. and T. N. Ingram, "Correlates of Salespeople Ethical Conflict: An Exploratory Investigation," *Journal of Business Ethics,* 3, 1984, p. 343–353; Dubinsky, A. J. and I. M. Gwin, "Business Ethics: Buyers and Sellers," *Journal of Purchasing and Materials Management,* Winter 1981, Vol. 17, p. 9–16.

◉

TRUST-BASED RELATIONSHIP SELLING
EXPERIENTIAL EXERCISE 2.5
Salesperson and Buyer Interviews

OBJECTIVE: You will gather information from a buyer and a seller about the activities associated with their job.

THE EXERCISE ASSIGNMENT

This exercise will familiarize you with the day-to-day activities of a salesperson and a buyer. Ideally, the exercise will carry even more meaning if you can call on a buyer and a seller from the same industry.

    To complete this exercise, you will first need to identify (a) a salesperson and (b) a buyer willing to talk with you about their job roles and activities. Use the following *Salesperson Interview Questions* and *Buyer Interview Questions* as a guide for interviewing both the salesperson and the buyer. Record the responses you receive during these interviews and use them to complete the two discussion questions which follow the interview questions. Your survey results and responses to the discussion questions will be handed in and used as inputs for class discussions comparing your results with those of other students in the class.

Salesperson Interview Questions

1. What industry are you in?

2. What is the formal title used to designate your position in the company?

    No. of years selling with the company _____

    No. of years total selling experience _____

3. How many hours per week do you work?

4. What percent of your typical week is spent in the following activities?
    a. Prospecting
    b. Administration (that is, paperwork)
    c. Travel

Harcourt Brace & Company

    d. Face-to-face selling

    e. Internal meetings

    f. Account service

5. In a sales presentation, what percent of your time is spent on the following activities?

    a. Information gathering

    b. Actual sales presentation

    c. Commitment (confirming, handling objections, closing)

    d. Follow through (servicing the account after the sale)

6. What preparations do you make before meeting with a prospective buyer?

7. On average, how many sales calls do you make to the same prospect in order to successfully make the sale?

8. What percent of your sales calls result in a sale?

9. How often do you talk with the buyer between sales?

10. On a scale of 1 = no stress to 10 = a great deal of stress, how stressful do you perceive your job? What do you find most stressful about your job?

11. On a scale of 1 = very negative to 10 = very positive, what do you believe are the customers' perceptions of the salespeople associated with your industry?

12. Do you eventually develop an opinion or attitude about a buyer and adjust your presentation accordingly or is it typical in your industry to use a fairly standard sales presentation?

13. What percent of your total compensation is salary, commission, and bonus? Does this compensation plan provide adequate incentive for you? How could the compensation plan be improved to enhance your motivation?

14. What abilities (characteristics) do you believe are crucial for success in your industry?

15. As you carry out your roles as a salesperson, how important are each of the following? Why are they perceived in this manner?

    a. Trust

    b. Communication

    c. Relationships

    d. Ethics

Harcourt Brace & Company

16. What college courses prepared you the most for your career in sales?

17. How often do you set goals for your sales calls? Are these formalized (that is, written)? Give me an example of a prospecting goal you would set. Give me an example of a selling goal you would set.

18. Do you keep formal records of sales calls? May I have a blank copy of your sales call report?

19. How much formal sales training does your organization provide? Is there a continuous sales training program in place? At what intervals do you participate in this training?

20. What aspects of your job do you enjoy most? What aspects do you enjoy least?

21. What is your most memorable sales call?

Buyer Interview Questions

1. What business or industry are you in?

2. What is the formal title used to designate your position in the company?

   No. of years in purchasing with this company _____

   No. of years total purchasing experience _____

3. How many hours per week do you work?

4. What percent of your typical week is spent in the following activities?
   a. Researching, identifying, and clarifying needs
   b. Specifying product requirements (quality, features, volume, and so on)
   c. Researching and identifying potential suppliers
   d. Requesting and acquiring sales proposals
   e. Evaluating proposals and selecting suppliers
   f. Evaluation of satisfaction with purchase
   g. Problem resolution
   h. Administration (that is, record keeping and paperwork)

5. As a buyer in a sales presentation, what percent of your time is spent on the following activities?
   a. Giving information
   b. Information gathering
   c. Negotiating details

6. As a buyer, what preparations do you make before meeting with a salesperson? How do these preparations differ between salespeople you currently buy from and salespeople from whom you are not already buying?

7. On average, how many sales meetings are required *with the same salesperson* before you make a purchase?

8. On average, how often do you talk with a salesperson between purchases from that salesperson or his or her company?

9. On a scale from 1 = no stress to 10 = a great deal of stress, how stressful do you perceive your job? What do you find most stressful about your job?

10. On a scale from 1 = very negative to 10 = very positive, what do you believe is the typical customer's perception of the salespeople associated with your industry?

11. What percent of your total compensation is salary, commission, and bonus? Does this compensation plan provide adequate incentive for you? How could the compensation plan be improved to enhance your motivation?

12. What abilities (characteristics) do you believe are crucial for success as a buyer?

13. What college courses prepared you the most for your career as a buyer?

14. Considering your experience as a buyer, what characteristics do you perceive as important in salespeople? Please rank the following items in order of importance (1 = most important, 2 = next most important, 8 = least important).

Aggressive   _____

Creative   _____

Disciplined   _____

Likable   _____

Knowledgeable   _____

Professional   _____

Verbally skilled   _____

Well-groomed   _____

15. What percent of your company's purchases requires the input of more than one person in the purchase decision?

16. What aspects of your job do you enjoy most? What aspects do you enjoy least?

17. As you carry out your role as a buyer dealing with different suppliers and salespeople, how important are each of the following? Why are they perceived in this manner?

   a. Trust
   b. Communication
   c. Relationships
   d. Ethics

18. What is your most memorable sales interaction with a salesperson?

19. What time of day do you find best to work with salespeople?

Discussion Questions

1. After you have interviewed your buyer and seller describe what characteristics appear to be essential to to be successful in each of these professions.

   a. Sales _____

   _____

   _____

   _____

   _____

   b. Buyer _____

   _____

   _____

   _____

   _____

Harcourt Brace & Company

2. If your salesperson or buyer perceived their job to be stressful, what made it so?

_____

_____

_____

_____

_____

_____

3. If your salesperson or buyer perceived their job not to be stressful, what made it so?

_____

_____

_____

_____

_____

_____

Harcourt Brace & Company

TRUST-BASED RELATIONSHIP SELLING
EXPERIENTIAL EXERCISE 2.6
Assessing the Lifetime Value of a Customer

OBJECTIVE: The lifeline of an organization is repeat business, obtained by keeping present customers happy. In this exercise you will calculate the value of a customer over a five-year period.

THE LIFETIME VALUE OF A CUSTOMER

Identify a salesperson with whom you can establish a rapport and working relationship that allows you to accompany or shadow the salesperson for a day. Note the various behaviors and activities the salesperson performs that have some relationship (good and bad) to the development and maintenance of buyer–seller relationships.

With the assistance of the salesperson, select one customer and calculate the lifetime value of that customer.

In a short report, present the relationship activities (good and bad) you observed during the shadowing opportunity, along with the lifetime value calculation. The report must contain explanation and support for the value determined.

As noted earlier, the lifeline of organizations today is repeat business. Present customers have already developed trust with their salesperson and, with proper nurturing, should be easier to sell to over time.

In the grocery industry, the average customer spends $100 per week for 50 weeks each year. The value of this customer each year is $5,000 and over five years, $25,000.

In the consumer goods industry (for example, Frito Lay, Mike Sell, Pringles), an average order from a small grocery store (independent grocer) is $1,000 per week. The value of this customer per year is $50,000 and over five years, $250,000.

THE EXERCISE ASSIGNMENT

1. Contact a salesperson and ask what an average customer would order per month. Calculate the value over five years for this customer.

    _____

    _____

    _____

Harcourt Brace & Company

_____

_____

_____

_____

_____

2. Discuss with the salesperson how much time it takes to develop this type of customer.

_____

_____

_____

_____

_____

_____

3. Discuss the implications of losing an active customer and how much time and effort it takes to replace a lost customer.

_____

_____

_____

_____

_____

_____

_____

Harcourt Brace & Company

4. Ask your salesperson the amount of effort it takes to get business from an existing account versus generating new business.

_____

_____

_____

_____

_____

_____

_____

_____

Harcourt Brace & Company

MODULE THREE

THE TRUST-BASED RELATIONSHIP SELLING PROCESS

In today's increasingly competitive marketplace, buyers typically find themselves inundated with choices regarding both products and suppliers. In this virtual buyers' market, traditional selling methods focused on closing the sale have been found to be inefficient and often counter-productive to the organization's larger, longer-term marketing strategy. In this new competitive environment, buyers are demanding unique solutions to their problems—product solutions that are customized on the basis of their particular problems and needs. Additionally, the adversarial, win-lose characteristics so customary in traditional selling are fading fast. In their place, longer-term buyer-seller relationships are evolving as the preferred form of doing business. While buyers are finding it more effective and efficient to do *more* business with *fewer* suppliers, sellers are finding it more effective to develop a continuing stream of business from the *right* customers than to continuously be searching for and calling on new prospects or having to re-sell previous customers.

This shift toward relationship selling has altered both the roles played by salespeople and the activities and skills they exercise in carrying out these roles—the selling process itself. Today's more contemporary selling process is embedded within the relationship marketing paradigm. As such, it emphasizes the initiation and nurturing of long-term buyer-seller relationships based on mutual trust and value-added benefits. The level of problem solving activity common to relationship selling requires deliberate and purposeful collaboration between both parties. These joint efforts are directed at creating unique solutions based on an enhanced knowledge and understanding of the customer's needs and the supplier's capabilities so that both parties derive mutual benefits. The nature of this integrative, win-win, and collaborative negotiation relies on augmented communication and interpersonal skills that nurture and sustain the reciprocal trust that allows all parties to fully share information and work together as a strategic problem solving team.

The following figure demonstrates the changing nature of activities making up the selling process as we shift from a transaction focus to a trust-based relationship orientation. As the figure illustrates, the skills and activities inherent to relationship selling can be

Harcourt Brace & Company

COMPARING THE TRADITIONAL TASK-FOCUSED SELLING AND THE TRUST-BASED RELATIONSHIP SELLING PROCESSES

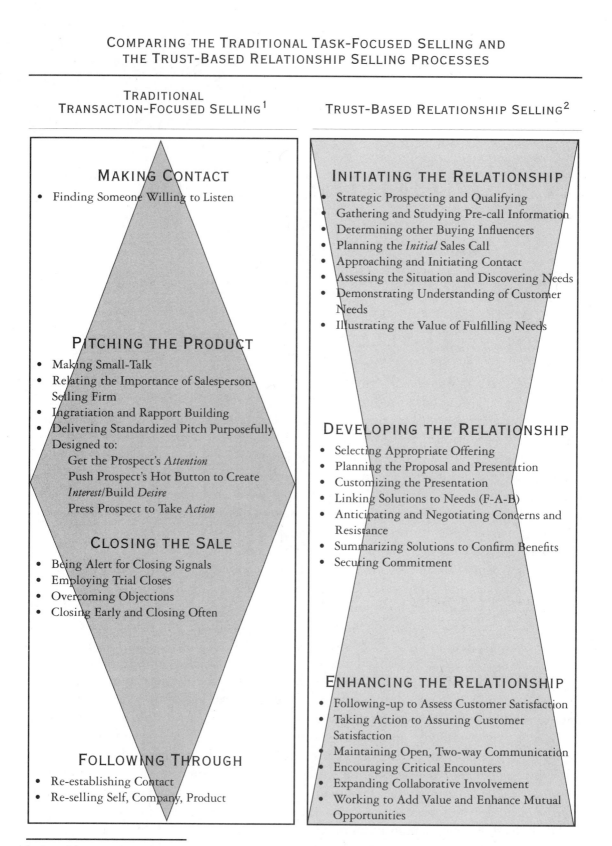

TRADITIONAL TRANSACTION-FOCUSED SELLING[1]

MAKING CONTACT

- Finding Someone Willing to Listen

PITCHING THE PRODUCT

- Making Small-Talk
- Relating the Importance of Salesperson-Selling Firm
- Ingratiation and Rapport Building
- Delivering Standardized Pitch Purposefully Designed to:
    Get the Prospect's *Attention*
    Push Prospect's Hot Button to Create *Interest*/Build *Desire*
    Press Prospect to Take *Action*

CLOSING THE SALE

- Being Alert for Closing Signals
- Employing Trial Closes
- Overcoming Objections
- Closing Early and Closing Often

FOLLOWING THROUGH

- Re-establishing Contact
- Re-selling Self, Company, Product

TRUST-BASED RELATIONSHIP SELLING[2]

INITIATING THE RELATIONSHIP

- Strategic Prospecting and Qualifying
- Gathering and Studying Pre-call Information
- Determining other Buying Influencers
- Planning the *Initial* Sales Call
- Approaching and Initiating Contact
- Assessing the Situation and Discovering Needs
- Demonstrating Understanding of Customer Needs
- Illustrating the Value of Fulfilling Needs

DEVELOPING THE RELATIONSHIP

- Selecting Appropriate Offering
- Planning the Proposal and Presentation
- Customizing the Presentation
- Linking Solutions to Needs (F-A-B)
- Anticipating and Negotiating Concerns and Resistance
- Summarizing Solutions to Confirm Benefits
- Securing Commitment

ENHANCING THE RELATIONSHIP

- Following-up to Assess Customer Satisfaction
- Taking Action to Assuring Customer Satisfaction
- Maintaining Open, Two-way Communication
- Encouraging Critical Encounters
- Expanding Collaborative Involvement
- Working to Add Value and Enhance Mutual Opportunities

[1]Adapted from T. Alessandra, P. Wexler, and R. Barrera, *Non-Manipulative Selling,* New York: Prentice Hall Press (1987).
[2]Adapted from T.N. Ingram and R.W. LaForge, *Sales Management: Analysis and Decision Making* (Fort Worth, TX, The Dryden Press, 1992).

Harcourt Brace & Company

classified according to their purpose as: (a) Initiation of the Relationship; (b) Development of the Relationship; and (c) Enhancement of the Relationship. As the activities comprising the selling process have changed, so too have the relative importance and degree of selling effort devoted to each stage of the process.

In the figure, the relative importance and emphasis placed on each of the primary selling activities is denoted by the width of the shaded geometric figure surrounding the activities. The traditional, task-focused salesperson places the greatest emphasis on convincing the customer to buy—making the presentation, closing, and overcoming objections. In contrast, the trust-based relationship selling process places the greatest importance and effort on (a) initiating the buyer-seller relationship through a sincere and deliberate effort of planning and information gathering directed at discovering the customer's needs; and (b) providing post-sale follow-up activities to assure satisfaction and further enhance mutual opportunities through expanded collaboration. Making the presentation, negotiating concerns and resistance, and gaining commitment are still important within the trust-based relationship selling process; however, they naturally flow out of the preceding activities of initiating the relationship and thus require less effort or emphasis. Similarly, presenting and gaining commitment in subsequent sales proposals are further facilitated by successful follow-through efforts targeted at enhancing the buyer-seller relationship.

The exercises in this module illustrate and build your skills in practicing relationship selling. Reflecting the critical importance of gathering and studying information about a specific buyer prior to making a call on that buyer, Experiential Exercise 3.1 (*Gathering Information About the Buyer*) is designed to assist you in determining what types of information are needed and where the information might be found. Exercise 3.2 (*Comparing the Traditional Selling Process with the Process of Trust-Based Relationship Selling*) walks you through a comparison of the transaction selling process and the process used in relationship selling. Understanding the differences and why these differences have evolved will assist you in applying the skills of relationship selling. Exercise 3.3 (*Building Relationships After the Sale*) builds your understanding of the process of servicing accounts by taking the service concepts and translating them into actual actions you might apply as you interact with both prospects and customers.

Harcourt Brace & Company

◉

THE TRUST-BASED RELATIONSHIP SELLING PROCESS
EXPERIENTIAL EXERCISE 3.1
Gathering Information about the Buyer

OBJECTIVE: You will understand why it is important to collect information about your prospect.

THE EXERCISE ASSIGNMENT

The more you know about your buyer, the better chance you have to sell. Over time you should be able to accumulate knowledge about your prospect. The information you will need varies with the kind of product you are selling. As a rule, you should definitely know a few basic things about your customers. A salesperson can learn a great deal about a customer over time by collecting bits and pieces of information, sorting them out, and developing a personalized, custom presentation for the customer.

The following information is helpful in preparing this personalized presentation.

1. The prospect's name, with correct spelling and correct pronunciation. Why is it important to know the correct spelling and pronunciation of your prospects name?

   _____

   _____

   _____

2. The prospect's correct title. Why is it important to know the correct title of your prospect?

   _____

   _____

   _____

3. The prospect's hobbies. Why is it important to know your prospect's hobbies?

   _____

   _____

   _____

Harcourt Brace & Company

4. The prospect's friends. Why is it important to know the names of your prospect's friends?

_____

_____

_____

5. The prospect's status in the community. Why is it important to know the prospect's status in the community?

_____

_____

_____

6. Things not to talk about with the prospect. Why is it important to know certain topics not to talk about with the prospect?

_____

_____

_____

7. The prospect's children. Why is it important to know the names and ages of your prospect's children?

_____

_____

_____

8. The prospect's favorite teams. Why is it important to know your prospect's favorite sports teams?

_____

_____

_____

Harcourt Brace & Company

Harvey Mackay in *Swim with the Sharks Without Being Eaten Alive* has his salesforce collect information on 66 items that profile their customers. Some of these include:

(1) Does the customer smoke?

(2) Spouse's education

(3) Graduated from what university?

(4) Belongs to clubs or service clubs

(5) Vacation habits

(6) Make and model of car they drive

Why is this type of information important to the salesperson?

_____

_____

_____

_____

_____

Points for Discussion

1. How can this information improve the communication process with the buyer?

_____

_____

_____

_____

2. How do you collect this information?

_____

_____

_____

_____

Harcourt Brace & Company

3. How long should it take you to collect this information?

    _____

    _____

    _____

    _____

4. What other types of information would be valuable to have?

    _____

    _____

    _____

    _____

THE TRUST-BASED RELATIONSHIP SELLING PROCESS
EXPERIENTIAL EXERCISES 3.2
Comparing the Traditional Selling Process with the Process of Trust-Based Relationship Selling

OBJECTIVE: To assist the student in acquiring a richer understanding of the differences between the traditional process of selling and the process inherent to trust-based relationship selling.

THE EXERCISE ASSIGNMENT

Study and discuss the activities comprising the traditional task-focused selling process and the trust-based relationship selling process as illustrated in the preceding introduction to this module. As you study these two processes, compare and contrast their component activities, their emphasis, and focus. Then complete the following study questions:

1. Compare and contrast these two processes of selling. How are they similar? How do they differ?

   _____

   _____

   _____

   _____

   _____

   _____

   _____

   _____

Harcourt Brace & Company

2. What is the primary focus of each of the two processes?

_____

_____

_____

_____

_____

_____

_____

_____

3. Why has the evolution toward trust-based relationship selling taken place? What has caused (is causing) this shift from one process to another?

_____

_____

_____

_____

_____

_____

_____

4. Explain what is meant by the different areas of emphasis as depicted by the shaded geometric figures overlaying each of the two processes.

_____

_____

_____

_____

_____

_____

_____

_____

Why would these differences in emphasis exist?

_____

_____

_____

5. What advantages are offered to the seller by trust-based relationship selling?

_____

_____

_____

_____

_____

_____

To the buyer?

_____

_____

_____

_____

Harcourt Brace & Company

6. What inherent disadvantages to the seller result from trust-based relationship selling?

_____

_____

_____

_____

_____

_____

_____

To the buyer?

_____

_____

_____

_____

_____

THE TRUST-BASED RELATIONSHIP SELLING PROCESS
EXPERIENTIAL EXERCISE 3.3
Building Relationships after the Sale

OBJECTIVE: You will discover the importance of follow-up activities in building relationships.

THE EXERCISE ASSIGNMENT

Not many years ago salespeople often thought their job was complete once the order was signed. Today, for a business to survive, repeat business is critical. A greater emphasis has been placed on the follow-up stage of the selling process. Continued building of the relationship should be your goal well after the sale.

1. Show appreciation after the sale. How might you accomplish this?

   _____

   _____

   _____

2. Monitor delivery and installation. Why is this important?

   _____

   _____

   _____

3. Learn the names of the switchboard operator, receptionists, office manager, users of the product, etc. How might you accomplish this and why is it important?

   _____

   _____

   _____

Harcourt Brace & Company

4. Keep all of your promises. How might you accomplish this and why is this important?

_____

_____

_____

5. Find ways to add value to your product or service. How might you accomplish this and why is it important?

_____

_____

_____

6. What should you try to accomplish during follow-up calls?

_____

_____

_____

Harcourt Brace & Company

MODULE FOUR

UNDERSTANDING BUYER EXPECTATIONS AND BEHAVIOR

As professional salespeople move from a transaction-focused to a trust-based, relationship selling orientation, it becomes increasingly important to understand what buyers expect and how they buy. Many organizational buyers want to work closely with a small number of suppliers. Therefore, what they expect from these suppliers and their salespeople is changing. Research indicates that most buyers prefer to do business with salespeople who are ethical, well-prepared, dependable, and imaginative in offering complete solutions to their problems. Understanding these new expectations and buying behavior is critical. Successful salespeople know the expectations and buying behavior of each buyer. They use this information to access the right people with the right information at the right stage in the buying process.

Experiential Exercise 4.1 (*What Buyers Expect from Salespeople*) will help you understand the basic expectations of most organizational buyers. You will have the opportunity to explain each of these expectations, translate each expectation into implications for salespeople, and present examples of how salespeople meet these expectations successfully.

Experiential Exercise 4.2 (*Triggering the Buying Process—Needs Awareness*) helps you explore different ways that the organizational buying process might be initiated. You will discuss how people inside and outside the buying organization might start the buying process and how a salesperson can trigger each source.

The organizational purchasing process typically incorporates many different people from different functions within the organization. Everyone participating in a particular buying process for a product or service is considered to be a member of the buying center for that process. Identifying the specific members of the buying center and understanding their degree of influence, needs, and expectations is extremely important for salespeople. Experiential Exercise 4.3 (*Working with a Buying Center*) addresses this key area. You will have the opportunity to identify buying center members, assess their level of influence in the buying process, and suggest their basic needs and expectations. Comparing the results across all buying center members will illustrate how salespeople must adapt to different individuals when selling a product or service to an organization.

Harcourt Brace & Company

Organizational buying situations have typically been classified into three categories: straight rebuy, modified rebuy, and new task. The buying process is somewhat different for each type of buying situation, usually becoming more complex when moving from a straight rebuy to a new task. In addition, the salesperson faces a different challenge depending upon whether she or he represents the in-vendor or an out-vendor. Experiential Exercise 4.4 (*Buying Situations and What to Do as an In-Vendor (Supplier) or Out-Vendor*) lets you propose different strategies for each buying situation type from an in-vendor and an out-vendor perspective.

The experiential exercises in Module Four should help you develop an understanding of the organizational buying process facing most salespeople. This understanding of buying expectations and behavior, the buying process, the buying center, and different buying situations is needed to be a successful salesperson in a trust-based, relationship environment. Successful salespeople typically adapt their strategies to reflect different buying situations, processes, and buying center members. In general, the more you know about an organization's buying process, the better the position you are in to develop a long-term, profitable relationship with the organization.

Harcourt Brace & Company

UNDERSTANDING BUYER EXPECTATIONS AND BEHAVIOR
EXPERIENTIAL EXERCISE 4.1
What Buyers Expect from Salespeople

OBJECTIVE: You will learn what buyers expect from salespeople, what these expectations really mean, and what implications they have for salesperson behaviors in working with customers.

Significant evidence indicates that buyers prefer to do business with a salesperson who:

- coordinates all aspects of the product/service mix to provide a total package.
- provides counseling to the customer based on in-depth knowledge of the product, the market, and the customer's needs.
- engages in problem solving with a high degree of proficiency that ensures satisfactory customer service over extended time periods.
- demonstrates high ethical standards and is honest in all communications.
- advocates the customer's wishes within the selling organization.
- is imaginative in meeting the buyer's needs.
- is well prepared for sales calls.
- is dependable; for example, he or she is punctual and follows up thoroughly.

THE EXERCISE ASSIGNMENT

Put yourself in the role of salesperson for National Computer Corporation. You are currently working to sell the College of Business at your university a large number of upgraded personal computers. These computers will be placed in staff and faculty offices for use with a variety of networking, wordprocessing, spreadsheet, and statistical analysis applications. The committee responsible for the purchase decision includes two faculty members and the Director of Purchasing for the univerity.

From the perspective of this buying situation, use the following pages to **explain** what each of the above buyer expectations means. **Discuss** the implications of each expectation and how it might influence your behavior. **Give an example** of how a salesperson might fulfill each buyer expectation.

Harcourt Brace & Company

1. Coordinates all aspects of the product/service mix to provide a total package.

_____

_____

_____

_____

_____

_____

_____

_____

2. Provides counseling based on knowledge of the product, the market, and the customer's needs.

_____

_____

_____

_____

_____

_____

_____

_____

Harcourt Brace & Company

3. Engages in problem solving with a high degree of proficiency that ensures satisfactory customer service over extended time periods.

_____

_____

_____

_____

_____

_____

_____

_____

4. Demonstrates high ethical standards and is honest in all communications.

_____

_____

_____

_____

_____

_____

_____

_____

Harcourt Brace & Company

5. Advocates the customer's wishes within the selling organization.

_____

_____

_____

_____

_____

_____

_____

_____

_____

_____

6. Is imaginative in meeting buyer's needs.

_____

_____

_____

_____

_____

_____

_____

_____

_____

Harcourt Brace & Company

7. Is well prepared for sales calls.

_____

_____

_____

_____

_____

_____

_____

_____

_____

_____

8. Is dependable.

_____

_____

_____

_____

_____

_____

_____

_____

_____

Harcourt Brace & Company

◉

UNDERSTANDING BUYER EXPECTATIONS AND BEHAVIOR
EXPERIENTIAL EXERCISE 4.2
Triggering the Buying Process— Needs Awareness

✳

OBJECTIVE: You will be able to determine both external and internal stimuli of the buying process needs recognition stage.

THE EXERCISE ASSIGNMENT

One of the most simple, yet far-reaching insights into buying behavior is that it is actually a *process.* There is a logical sequence of stages which collectively result in product and vendor choices. The salesperson is most concerned with *who* triggers stage one and *how* it becomes activated. As described by Hutt and Speh (1995), the eight sequential stages comprising the organizational buyer's decision process are as follows:

Stage 1. Anticipation or recognition of a problem (need) and a general solution

Stage 2. Determination of characteristics and quantity of needed item

Stage 3. Description of characteristics and quantity of needed item

Stage 4. Search for and qualification of potential source

Stage 5. Acquisition and analysis of proposal

Stage 6. Evaluation of proposals and selection of supplier(s)

Stage 7. Selection of order routine

Stage 8. Performance feedback and evaluation

The buying process begins when someone realizes a problem can be solved or an opportunity can be met by purchasing a product or service. This needs recognition can be initiated by either internal or external stimuli.

Assume that you are a salesperson for Sharp Business Equipment. An existing account, Performance Services International, has expressed interest in updating its

Harcourt Brace & Company

Hutt, M.D. and T.W. Speh, *Business Marketing Management,* Fifth Edition (Fort Worth, TX: The Dryden Press, 1995).

office and communications equipment. With the understanding that needs can be initiated by internal as well as external cues and stimuli, you have been working with the central purchasing office to develop better recognition and understanding of the company's needs and potential solutions.

Use the following worksheet to identify internal and external stimuli or cues that might arouse anticipation or recognition of a problem or need and initiate the buying process.

Internal Stimuli:

E
X   _Accounting department requests FAX machine_. How might this source be triggered?
A   _Salesperson meets with and works with different members of the accounting department_
M   _and demontrates the usefulness and benefits of a fax._
P   _____
L
E   _____

1. _____. How might this source be triggered?

    _____

    _____

    _____

2. _____. How might this source be triggered?

    _____

    _____

    _____

3. _____. How might this source be triggered?

    _____

    _____

    _____

4. _____. How might this source be triggered?

    _____

    _____

    _____

External Stimuli:

E
X *Data processing department sees ad in trade publication.* How might this source be triggered?
A
M *Understanding that members of the data processing department are exploring the*
P
L *benefits of using a fax machine, salesperson leaves several trade publications in the*
E
office for them to read.

1. _____. How might this source be triggered?

_____

_____

_____

2. _____. How might this source be triggered?

_____

_____

_____

3. _____. How might this source be triggered?

_____

_____

_____

4. _____. How might this source be triggered?

_____

_____

_____

UNDERSTANDING BUYER EXPECTATIONS AND BEHAVIOR
EXPERIENTIAL EXERCISE 4.3
Working with a Buying Center

OBJECTIVE: You will become sensitive to the many roles played by the various members of a buying center and how these roles often represent different problems, needs, and expectations that the salesperson must address.

INTRODUCTION

As products become increasingly complex, buying centers are becoming more prevalent in the marketplace. Buying centers present the salesperson with additional challenges, as she or he must determine:

1. who participates in buying a specific product or product category.
2. what role (user, influencer, buyer, decider, gatekeeper) each participant performs and the relative influence of that role.
3. what needs and expectations each participant has.
4. how to best discover and satisfy the needs and expectations of each buying center member.

THE EXERCISE ASSIGNMENT

As a salesperson for Candoo Computer Corporation (CCC), you have just received a call from your regional manager regarding a program now under way at one of your key accounts, Farmland Companies. Farmland is a national insurance company with agency offices spread across the United States. The company is in the early stages of designing and specifying a computer system that will place a computer in each agency office. The system will allow each agency to develop, operate, and maintain its own customer data base in order to provide better service to customers. In addition, by linking through the CCC mainframe, agencies, regional offices, and CCC headquarters will be networked for improved internal communications and access to corporate data bases.

You have serviced this account for several years and CCC equipment accounts for the biggest share of computers now in place at Farmland—some 35 to 40 percent of all units. As reflected in your share of this account's business, you and CCC have a good reputation and strong relationship with Farmland. In talking with Aimee Linn, your usual contact in the Farmland purchasing office, you have learned that this agency network system is the

Harcourt Brace & Company

brainstorm and pet project of Mike Hughes, a very "hands-on" CEO. Consequently, the probability of the system becoming a reality is very high. While faxing a complete set of hardware specs to you, Aimee has also let you know that, although Kerri Nicks, director of the Farmland MIS Department, is actually heading up this project, the national agency sales director, Tim Long, is also very active in its design and requirement specification. His interest stems not only from wanting to make sure the system will do what is needed at the corporate, regional, and agency levels, but also from the fact that he brainstormed and spearheaded a similar project two years ago that was never implemented. The previous effort did not have the blessing of Nicks in the MIS Department and it became a political football between the two departments. Each department wanted something different and both sides accused the other of not knowing what it was doing. Primarily because the CEO has commanded that it will be done, both sides seem to be playing ball with each other this time.

Aimee did hint at one concern, however: although corporate is designing and specifying the system, each agency has to purchase its units out of its own funds. Although the agencies exclusively represent only Farmland Insurance products, each agency is owned by the general agent—not Farmland. Some of the agents are not convinced that the system is worth the projected price tag of $3,500 per system, and Farmland cannot force them to buy the systems.

As with other selling opportunities with Farmland, this has all the makings of a decision that will be made as a result of multiple inputs from an assortment of individuals across the company—a buying center of sorts. As the salesperson having primary responsibility for this account, how would you go about identifying the various members of the buying center? Using the worksheet provided:

1. Identify each member of the buying center and the role each participant plays, and estimate the amount of influence (low, medium, high, very high) each has on the final decision.

2. What are the major problems, needs, and expectations that you will need to address for each of these buying center members?

As you complete this assignment, remember that a single individual can perform multiple roles in the center. Furthermore, it is common to find more than one individual playing the same buying center role.

Harcourt Brace & Company

Harcourt Brace & Company

IDENTIFICATION OF BUYING CENTER MEMBERS

BUYING CENTER ROLE	MEMBER PLAYING THIS ROLE	MEMBER'S INFLUENCE	MEMBER'S PERCEIVED NEEDS AND EXPECTATIONS
Users			
Influencers			
Buyers			
Deciders			
Gatekeepers			

UNDERSTANDING BUYER EXPECTATIONS AND BEHAVIOR
EXPERIENTIAL EXERCISE 4.4
Buying Situations and What to Do as an In-Vendor (Supplier) or Out-Vendor

OBJECTIVE: You will understand that different strategies will have to be used depending on the buying situation and whether you are an in-vendor or out-vendor.

THE EXERCISE ASSIGNMENT

Straight Rebuy. A buying situation in which the customer is basically reordering an item already in use. Little or nothing has changed in terms of product, price, delivery, the available sources of supply, or any other aspect. This is a low-risk situation involving little cognitive effort and requiring little information. The purchasing department or a clerical person is often the key influence of the decision maker.

What do you need to do as an in-vendor to keep this business?

Explain _____

_____

_____

What do you need to do as an out-vendor to get your foot in the door and persuade this company to buy from you?

Explain _____

_____

_____

Modified Rebuy. A buying situation in which the customer is already purchasing the item, but some key aspect has changed. For example, there may be a proposed price change, a new competitive source of supply, a problem with delivery, a change in product specifications, a newly available product feature or service, or a substitute product. These are moderate-risk situations requiring greater effort and necessitating better information and information sources.

Harcourt Brace & Company

What do you need to do as an in-vendor to keep this business?

Explain _____

_____

_____

What do you need to do as an out-vendor to get your foot in the door and persuade this company to buy from you?

Explain _____

_____

_____

New Task. Here the customer is buying something for the first time. He or she needs to be educated about products and vendors. The risk is great, the effort required is extensive, and the need to develop an information base is most pressing. The purchasing department often plays only a small role.

How do your strategies change for a new task prospect? _____

_____

_____

_____

Harcourt Brace & Company

MODULE FIVE

COMMUNICATION SKILLS

Effective communication skills are needed to identify buying needs and to indicate to buyers how a salesperson's company can satisfy those needs better than competitors. Communication skills are important throughout all stages of the trust-based relationship selling process presented in Module Three. Different communication skills are required at different stages of the selling process. We focus on general communication in this module and then specific communications skills in subsequent modules.

Experiential Exercise 5.1 (*Assessing Salesperson Communication*) provides an opportunity to investigate various aspects of salesperson communication. You will evaluate several statements concerning salesperson communication and then discuss what salespeople need to do if they are to communicate successfully with buyers.

Although we typically think of verbal communication in a sales situation, nonverbal communication is also extremely important. Salespeople need to be able to identify and interpret the nonverbal communication of buyers and to make sure their nonverbal communication is effective. Experiential Exercise 5.2 (*Interpreting Nonverbal Communication*) will give you practice in observing nonverbal communication and interpreting what it means.

The traditional transaction selling model was based on one-way communication between buyer and seller. The salesperson did the talking and the buyer listened and occasionally responded. A trust-based, relationship selling orientation is built on a foundation of mutual benefit. Therefore, communication is a two-way street with the buyer and seller involved in a "sales conversation" to ensure that both understand each other. Experiential Exercise 5.3 (*One-way Communication*) and Experiential Exercise 5.4 (*Two-way Communication*) illustrate these two different approaches. After completing these exercises, you should be convinced of the value of two-way communication and the need for a salesperson to involve the buyer in a conversation rather than a one-way monologue.

Research has consistently found that most individuals have a typical communication style. Communication is most effective when both individuals employ the same style. Thus, there is not one communication style that is best. Nevertheless it is important for

Harcourt Brace & Company

communication styles to match for communication to be the most effective. In a sales situation it is important for the salesperson to know their typical communication style and the communication style of those involved in the buying process. Experiential Exercise 5.5. (*Communication Styles: A Self-Assessment*) will let you evaluate your particular communication style and the communication styles of others. You will classify yourself and others as either having an amiable, expressive, analytical, or driver communication style.

It is the salesperson's job to adapt their communication style to that of the buyer. Experiential Exercise 5.6 (*Style Flexibility: Adapting Interpersonal Communication Styles*) investigates how a salesperson with one particular communication style must adjust to communicate effectively with buyers having different styles.

The communications skills developed in Module Five should help you in all types of interpersonal communication. These skills are especially important for salespeople trying to develop trust-based, relationships with customers. However, they are also important in communicating effectively with people in an organization.

Harcourt Brace & Company

COMMUNICATION SKILLS
EXPERIENTIAL EXERCISE 5.1
Assessing Salesperson Communication

OBJECTIVE: You will become aware of the importance of communication in developing buyer–seller strategies.

THE EXERCISE ASSIGNMENT

Read each of the following statements. Determine which are true and which are false about the benefits that good listening can bring about in business relationships.

True or False

_____   1. Skill in listening improves your self-confidence.

          Rationale: _____

          _____

          _____

_____   2. Customers like you when you listen to them.

          Rationale: _____

          _____

          _____

_____   3. Good listeners are usually more efficient in completing their work.

          Rationale: _____

          _____

          _____

Harcourt Brace & Company

_____ 4. What you create with good listening is flexibility in settling
disagreements.

Rationale: _____

_____

_____

_____ 5. Intelligent responses are easier when you listen.

Rationale: _____

_____

_____

_____ 6. More decisions are made by "shooting from the hip" than by
listening to the opinions of your customers.

Rationale: _____

_____

_____

_____ 7. Learning to listen to customers helps you respond more quickly to
their needs.

Rationale: _____

_____

_____

_____ 8. Few good listeners are promoted to top management positions.

Rationale: _____

_____

_____

Harcourt Brace & Company

_____   9. Good listeners are not often embarrassed by unnecessary mistakes.

Rationale: _____

_____

_____

_____ 10. Handling distractions is difficult for good listeners.

Rationale: _____

_____

_____

_____ 11. Being an effective communicator is an essential qualification for a successful salesperson.

Rationale: _____

_____

_____

_____ 12. A good definition of communication is the sending of information from the salesperson to the buyer.

Rationale: _____

_____

_____

_____ 13. A salesperson who knows a subject well is, therefore, able to communicate it effectively.

Rationale: _____

_____

_____

Harcourt Brace & Company

_____ 14. The use of an example is a very good way for a salesperson to make
           a communication clear to their buyer.

           Rationale: _____

           _____

           _____

_____ 15. If customers do not understand, they will usually indicate lack of
           understanding by asking questions or by saying they don't
           understand.

           Rationale: _____

           _____

           _____

_____ 16. Most people can listen approximately three times as fast as they
           usually speak.

           Rationale: _____

           _____

           _____

_____ 17. Silence on the part of the customer usually indicates understanding
           and acceptance of the communication.

           Rationale: _____

           _____

           _____

Source: Bone, D., *The Business of Listening: A Practical Guide to Effective Listening* (Los Altos, CA: Crisp Publications, 1988).

Harcourt Brace & Company

COMMUNICATION SKILLS
EXPERIENTIAL EXERCISE 5.2
Interpreting Nonverbal Communication

OBJECTIVE: You will become aware of the vast amount of nonverbal communication that occurs and you will be able to interpret its meaning.

THE EXERCISE ASSIGNMENT

Research indicates that successful salespeople pick out and comprehend a high number of behavioral cues from the buyer. In addition, evidence shows that 50 percent or more of the meaning conveyed within the communication process stems from nonverbal behavior. These two factors underscore the importance of recognizing and interpreting nonverbal behaviors. This exercise is designed to help you practice identifying and understanding nonverbal communication through watching a video tape and participating in class discussion.

With your classmates, form several small work/discussion groups. These groups are useful for two reasons. First, the exercise encourages competition between the groups, thus increasing your active involvement. Second, discussing your perceptions of nonverbal cues and their meaning in a small group will facilitate the subsequent class discussion.

Turn to the worksheet on pages 84–85, tear out the pages, and write your name on them. These individual worksheets should be used **as you watch the video** to record nonverbal cues from both the buyer and the seller as you observe them. You can then use the sheet as input for the following small group and class discussions. Your instructor may ask you to turn in your worksheet at the end of class.

As you watch the video, remember to pick out nonverbal communication from both the buyer and the seller and make notes on your worksheet. Your instructor may choose to turn the audio up so you can hear the dialogue, or turn it down so you will have no verbal cues available for interpretation.

After watching the video, compare your results to those of the other members of your small group and discuss their meaning. Choose one individual in your group to be the group leader and spokesperson. This individual is responsible for combining the individual lists into a single list and tallying the total number of different nonverbal cues identified by your group.

After you have pooled your individual "sightings" and thoroughly interpreted and discussed their meaning, discuss your findings with the class. Which group identified the most nonverbal communications? Who missed what? This comparison usually turns into a lively and competitive discussion in which you can debate what the various nonverbal behaviors might have meant and the consequences of missing this communication on the part of the buyer or seller.

INTERPRETING NONVERBAL COMMUNICATION

Name: _____ Date: _____

During this exercise, your instructor will play a video tape. As the tape is being shown, use this worksheet to record any nonverbal communication you observe. After the video is played, meet with your discussion group to interpret the meaning of observed nonverbal communications and to compare the differences between individual choices. Groups will compare results to see who picked out the most nonverbal behaviors.

NONVERBAL COMMUNICATION OBSERVED	MEANING OF NONVERBAL COMMUNICATION

Harcourt Brace & Company

(continued on next page)

Harcourt Brace & Company

NONVERBAL COMMUNICATION OBSERVED

MEANING OF NONVERBAL COMMUNICATION

COMMUNICATION SKILLS
EXPERIENTIAL EXERCISE 5.3
One-way Communication

OBJECTIVE: You will be able to demonstrate the problems with one-way communication.

THE EXERCISE ASSIGNMENT

In this exercise, you will be asked to draw several geometric figures on the following worksheet page. These figures will be described to you by one of your classmates acting as a presenter. **In this particular exercise, the class is not allowed to ask any questions.** This exercise attempts to demonstrate traditional old-style selling where the salesperson talked at (as opposed to with) the buyer.

Compare your drawings to those of your classmates. Some drawings will closely resemble the presenter's description while others may match little, if any, of the original picture.

If you are speaking *at* a customer, your message may end up like this picture. Some customers will get it, others won't. Those buyers who do not get it will often wait for a salesperson (the competition?) who can explain their product so they understand it.

Harcourt Brace & Company

Harcourt Brace & Company

COMMUNICATION SKILLS
EXPERIENTIAL EXERCISE 5.4
Two-way Communication

OBJECTIVE: You will be able to demonstrate two-way communication and the benefits that result from feedback.

THE EXERCISE ASSIGNMENT

You will be asked to draw several figures. **The class *is* allowed to ask questions.**

   At the end of the presentation, your pictures should closely resemble the presenter's. Even with two-way communication, potential for error exists, which is why a salesperson uses visuals to enhance the communication process.

Harcourt Brace & Company

Harcourt Brace & Company

COMMUNICATION SKILLS
EXPERIENTIAL EXERCISE 5.5
Communication Styles: A Self-Assessment

OBJECTIVE: You will evaluate and understand your own style of interpersonal communication and further understand how this style differs from individual to individual.

THE EXERCISE ASSIGNMENT

Before reading the assigned material dealing with communication styles, complete the communication styles survey. Respond to the items in class, place your name in the proper location, and turn in the completed survey instrument. After completing your self-report, have a close friend fill out the duplicate survey titled Friend's Assessment.

   Using the instructions provided at the bottom of each assessment page, score both your self-assessment and the assessment of your style as evaluated by your friend. Plot these scores on the Communication Style Plotting Chart provided at the end of this exercise.

   Utilizing these plots, identify your Communication Style.

> Are you primarily a Driver/Director, an Expressive/Emotive, an Amiable/Supportive, or an Analytical/Reflective?

> What personal characteristics lead to your being depicted as this style?

> How well does your self-scored style correspond with the style indicated by your friend? If these are different, what might be contributing causes?

> What are the implications of your communication style in terms of interacting with others?

Harcourt Brace & Company

COMMUNICATION STYLE ASSESSMENT

Student Self-Assessment

Please complete this self-assessment of your interpersonal communication style. Circle the number that best represents your self-evaluation regarding each of the paired characteristics shown on the following two pages. Please give your candid reaction—there is no right or wrong answer.

I perceive myself as being . . .

Cooperative	1	2	3	4	5	Competitive
Submissive	1	2	3	4	5	Authoritarian
Accommodating	1	2	3	4	5	Domineering
Hesitant	1	2	3	4	5	Decisive
Reserved	1	2	3	4	5	Outgoing
Compromising	1	2	3	4	5	Insistent
Cautious	1	2	3	4	5	Risk-Taking
Patient	1	2	3	4	5	Hurried
Complacent	1	2	3	4	5	Influential
Quiet	1	2	3	4	5	Talkative
Shy	1	2	3	4	5	Bold
Supportive	1	2	3	4	5	Demanding
Relaxed	1	2	3	4	5	Tense
Restrained	1	2	3	4	5	Assertive

Scoring This Page Only:

- Add the circled numbers on this page and enter the sum here: _____

- Divide this sum by 14 to compute your Dominance Score: _____

Harcourt Brace & Company

I perceive myself as being . . .

Disciplined	1	2	3	4	5	Easy-Going
Controlled	1	2	3	4	5	Expressive
Serious	1	2	3	4	5	Light-Hearted
Methodical	1	2	3	4	5	Unstructured
Calculating	1	2	3	4	5	Spontaneous
Guarded	1	2	3	4	5	Open
Stalwart	1	2	3	4	5	Humorous
Aloof	1	2	3	4	5	Friendly
Formal	1	2	3	4	5	Casual
Reserved	1	2	3	4	5	Attention-Seeking
Cautious	1	2	3	4	5	Carefree
Conforming	1	2	3	4	5	Unconventional
Reticent	1	2	3	4	5	Dramatic
Restrained	1	2	3	4	5	Impulsive

Scoring This Page Only:

- Add the circled numbers on this page and enter the sum here: _____
- Divide this sum by 14 to compute your Sociability Score: _____

AFTER SCORING BOTH PAGES, PLOT YOUR DOMINANCE AND SOCIABILITY SCORES ON THE COMMUNICATION STYLE PLOT (P.96).

Harcourt Brace & Company

COMMUNICATION STYLE ASSESSMENT

Friend's Assessment

_____ has selected you as someone who would be familiar with his or her interpersonal communication style. Please complete this assessment of that individual's interpersonal communication style by circling the number that best represents your evaluation regarding each of the paired characteristics shown on the following two pages. Please give your candid reaction—there is no right or wrong answer.

I perceive this person as being . . .

Cooperative	1	2	3	4	5	Competitive
Submissive	1	2	3	4	5	Authoritarian
Accommodating	1	2	3	4	5	Domineering
Hesitant	1	2	3	4	5	Decisive
Reserved	1	2	3	4	5	Outgoing
Compromising	1	2	3	4	5	Insistent
Cautious	1	2	3	4	5	Risk-Taking
Patient	1	2	3	4	5	Hurried
Complacent	1	2	3	4	5	Influential
Quiet	1	2	3	4	5	Talkative
Shy	1	2	3	4	5	Bold
Supportive	1	2	3	4	5	Demanding
Relaxed	1	2	3	4	5	Tense
Restrained	1	2	3	4	5	Assertive

Harcourt Brace & Company

I perceive this person as being . . .

	1	2	3	4	5	
Disciplined	1	2	3	4	5	Easy-Going
Controlled	1	2	3	4	5	Expressive
Serious	1	2	3	4	5	Light-Hearted
Methodical	1	2	3	4	5	Unstructured
Calculating	1	2	3	4	5	Spontaneous
Guarded	1	2	3	4	5	Open
Stalwart	1	2	3	4	5	Humorous
Aloof	1	2	3	4	5	Friendly
Formal	1	2	3	4	5	Casual
Reserved	1	2	3	4	5	Attention-Seeking
Cautious	1	2	3	4	5	Carefree
Conforming	1	2	3	4	5	Unconventional
Reticent	1	2	3	4	5	Dramatic
Restrained	1	2	3	4	5	Impulsive

THANK YOU FOR COMPLETING
THIS ASSESSMENT

Harcourt Brace & Company

Sources: David W. Merrill and Roger H. Reid, *Personal Styles and Effective Performance* (Radnor, PA: Chilton Book Company, 1981), and Gerald L. Manning and Barry L. Reece, *Selling Today: An Extension of the Marketing Concept* (Boston: Allyn and Bacon, 1995).

COMMUNICATION STYLE PLOT

Use this chart to plot your communication style.

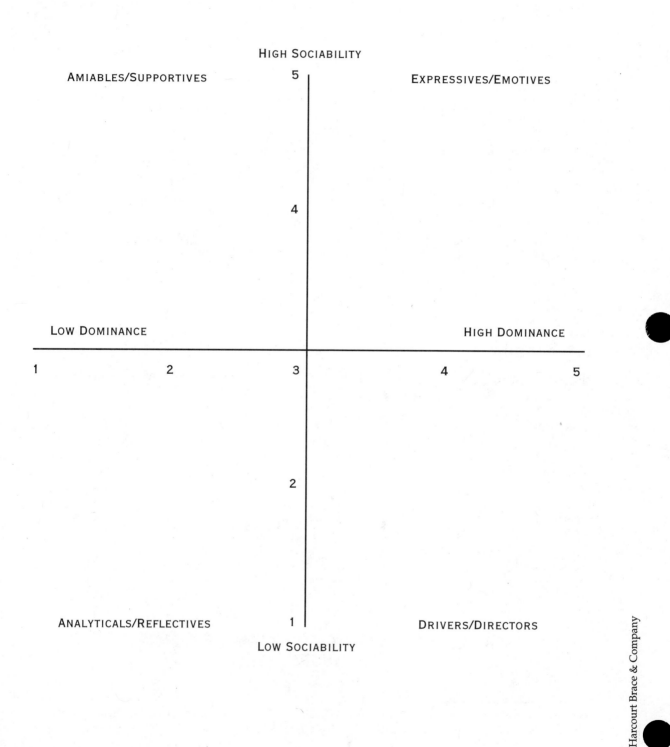

◉

COMMUNICATIONS SKILLS
EXPERIENTIAL EXERCISE 5.6
Style Flexibility: Adapting Interpersonal Communication Styles

✳

OBJECTIVE: You will understand how your interpersonal communication style might be flexed or adapted in order to better relate to buyers.

THE EXERCISE ASSIGNMENT

Based on your understanding of (a) interpersonal communication styles as discussed in class materials and (b) your personal communication style identified in the preceding exercise, respond to each of the following questions. These questions refer to how and why you would flex your style to better relate to buyers characterized by various communication styles.

My predominant interpersonal communication style is _____

1. What preparations and style flexing would you make in order to better relate to and communicate with customers characterized as **Drivers/Directors?**

_____

_____

_____

_____

_____

_____

_____

_____

_____

2. What preparations and style flexing would you make in order to better relate to and communicate with customers characterized as **Analyticals/Reflectives**?

_____

_____

_____

_____

_____

_____

_____

_____

_____

3. What preparations and style flexing would you make in order to better relate to and communicate with customers characterized as **Expressives/Emotives**?

_____

_____

_____

_____

_____

_____

_____

_____

_____

Harcourt Brace & Company

4. What preparations and style flexing would you make in order to better relate to and communicate with customers characterized as **Amiables/Supportives**?

_____

_____

_____

_____

_____

_____

_____

_____

_____

MODULE SIX

QUESTIONING SKILLS

One of the most important communication skills for salespeople is questioning skills. Asking the right questions at the right time helps salespeople identify needed information about the organization's buying process. This ensures that the buyer understands what the salesperson is communicating. Developing and asking effective questions requires planning and practice.

Experiential Exercise 6.1 (*Key Questions During the Buying Process*) focuses on the types of questions that might be asked at different stages of the buying process. You will examine various questions and determine why each question is important.

Experiential Exercise 6.2 (*Effective Questioning*) provides an opportunity to examine how open-ended and closed-ended questions are used in a sales interaction. You will view a sales call and identify the types of questions used as well as the types of information gathered from these questions.

The planning of a general questioning strategy can be an effective approach to actively engage a buyer during a sales interaction. The ADAPT Process is one approach that can be used in many selling situations. The ADAPT Process emphasizes specific types of questions to help a buyer identify problems and needs. The specific types of questions include:

ASSESSMENT QUESTIONS:	questions to elicit factual information about the buyer's current situation
DISCOVERY QUESTIONS:	questions designed to uncover problems or dissatisfactions the buyer is experiencing
ACTIVATION QUESTIONS:	questions used to show the negative impact of a problem uncovered from the discovery questions
PROJECTION QUESTIONS:	questions designed to help the buyer determine the value of solving the identified problem

Harcourt Brace & Company

TRANSITION QUESTIONS: questions to confirm the buyer's desire to solve the identified problem

One of the major advantages of the ADAPT Process is that the questions help the buyer examine the current situation, identify problems, assess the negative impact of these problems, and calculate the value of solving these problems. The salesperson uses the questions to help the buyer through the process and does not try to sell the buyer a solution until transition questions are used. These questions help to make a smooth transition into a sales presentation.

The remaining exercises in this module provide various types of practice in using the ADAPT Process. Experiential Exercise 6.3 (*The ADAPT Questioning Process for Needs Discovery*) lets you develop general assessment, discovery, activation, projection, and transition questions. Experiential Exercise 6.4 (*Activating the ADAPT Process for Developing and Confirming Customer Needs*) gives you the opportunity to develop ADAPT questions for a particular selling situation. Experiential Exercise 6.5 (*Role Plays for ADAPTive Questioning Part I*) and Experiential Exercise 6.6 (*Role Plays for ADAPTive Questioning Part II*) allow you to plan and execute the ADAPT Process in two different role play situations. You get to actually ask the questions in a life-like selling situation and adapt to the situation depending upon the buyer's responses.

Questioning skills are extremely important in a trust-based, relationship process. Effective questions can uncover very useful information from buyers and ensure that buyers understand all aspects of the seller's offering. Successful salespeople continually work to improve their questioning skills.

QUESTIONING SKILLS
EXPERIENTIAL EXERCISE 6.1
Key Questions during the Buying Process

OBJECTIVE: You will be able to understand the importance of good, effective questioning.

THE EXERCISE ASSIGNMENT

During the buying process, the salesperson must always be gathering pertinent information. Answers to the following questions will help the sales rep identify the key individuals in a buying center and devise a strategy to penetrate the buying process. These questions should be asked of the various individuals the sales rep meets within a company.

1. Who, besides you, will be making the decision to buy? Explain why this question is important._____

   _____

   _____

2. What problems do you foresee in changing suppliers? Explain why this question is important. _____

   _____

   _____

3. What will you need to do to win the support of the others? Explain why this question is important. _____

   _____

   _____

Harcourt Brace & Company

4. When would you plan to make the purchase decision? Explain why this question is important. _____

    _____

    _____

5. What sense of urgency do you feel about this buying decision? Explain why this question is important. _____

    _____

    _____

6. Other important questions? _____

    _____

    Why? _____

Harcourt Brace & Company

◉

QUESTIONING SKILLS
EXPERIENTIAL EXERCISE 6.2
Effective Questioning

OBJECTIVE: You will understand the importance of asking effective questions.

INTRODUCTION

There are two ways to dominate or control a sales conversation. A salesperson can talk all the time, or the salesperson can be in control by asking good, effective questions. Effective questioning offers the salesperson the following advantages:

1. Questions establish an atmosphere of control.

2. Questions help you determine how cooperative your customer will be.

3. Questions get you valuable information about your customer's needs, desires, and problems.

4. Questions help you identify your customer's style and opinions as well as his or her current understanding and awareness of needs and of your product or service.

5. Questions help you avoid rejection.

6. Questions build trust and rapport.

7. Questions save you time.

8. Questions keep you from talking too much.

9. Questions get the customer involved.

10. Questions get and maintain the customer's attention.

11. Questions make your customer think.

12. Questions and subsequent answers, if you listen attentively, create a willingness on the part of the customer to listen to you when it is your turn to talk.

13. Intelligent questions make you look competent and knowledgeable.

A salesperson can use open-ended and closed-ended questions for effective questioning.

Open-ended and Closed-ended Questions

Open-ended Questions—Open-ended questions, also called nondirective questions, are designed to let the customer respond freely. That is, the customer is not limited to one- or two-word answers, and is encouraged to disclose personal and/or business information. These questions are typically used to probe the customer for descriptive information that allows the salesperson to better understand the specific needs of the customer.

Closed-ended Questions—Closed-ended questions, also called directive questions, are designed to limit the customer's response to one or two words. Although the most common form is the yes/no question, closed-ended questions can come in many forms—provided the response is limited to one or two words. For instance, "How many . . .", and "How often . . ." are examples of closed-ended questions. These questions are typically used to confirm or clarify information gleaned from responses to open-ended questions.

THE EXERCISE ASSIGNMENT

Used in combination, open- and closed-ended questions help the salesperson uncover and confirm customer needs, dissatisfactions, and opportunities. Let's look now at how these questions are used in the ADAPT process.

1. Observe a salesperson during an introductory call with a new prospect. What open-ended questions did the salesperson use?

    a. _____

    b. _____

    c. _____

    d. _____

    e. _____

    What types of information were gathered using open-ended questions. After the sales call, ask the salesperson how he or she will use this information?

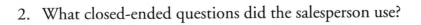

2. What closed-ended questions did the salesperson use?

    a. _____

    b. _____

    c. _____

    d. _____

    e. _____

    What types of information were gathered using closed-ended questions?
    After the sales call, ask the salesperson how he or she will use this
    information.

    _____

    _____

    _____

    _____

    _____

    _____

Harcourt Brace & Company

◎

QUESTIONING SKILLS
EXPERIENTIAL EXERCISE 6.3
*The ADAPT Questioning Process
for Needs Discovery*

OBJECTIVE: You will understand the "listen, comprehend, cognitively respond" nature of reactive listening while applying the ADAPT process for needs discovery.

THE EXERCISE ASSIGNMENT

This exercise involves a salesperson representing the direct sales department of American Seating Company (ASC) and a buyer with the Seattle Music Arts Association (SMAA).

Although there are some 12 manufacturers of auditorium seating, ASC's market share of 21 percent makes the company a leader in this industry. ASC's selling efforts are organized on a basis of market types: One department sells to end users and a second department sells to distributors who in turn sell to retailers of business furniture. Direct sales to end users are restricted to minimum orders of $200, 000.

As an integral part of a major remodeling project, SMAA wants to replace the seats in the Seattle Metropolitan Auditorium. ASC estimates a potential sale of between $350,000 and $500,000. This range represents differences in both quantity and types of seating desired. According to industry sources, funding for this remodeling project is being provided through a bond issue. From this very basic knowledge of the buyer's situation, the salesperson is working through the ADAPT process with the buyer in order to better identify and confirm the actual needs for seating.

Using the ADAPT process (described on the following page) as a guide, work with your learning team to develop a scripted series of reactive salesperson questions and buyer responses that might be typical of this selling situation.

For your convenience and as a guide for completing this assignment, a sample **ADAPT Questioning Script Template** is included along with an **ADAPT Questioning Script Worksheet** on the following pages.

Harcourt Brace & Company

THE ADAPT PROCESS

ASSESSMENT QUESTIONS:

Questions designed to elicit factual information about the customer's current situation. These questions do not seek conclusions; rather, they seek information that describes the customer and his or her business environment. The information sought should augment or confirm pre-call research.

DISCOVERY QUESTIONS:

Questions designed to uncover problems or dissatisfactions the customer is experiencing that the salesperson's product or company may be able to solve. Basically, these questions are used to "discover" or "boil down" the information gained from assessment questions and from pre-call research into *suggested* needs.

ACTIVATION QUESTIONS:

Questions used to show the negative impact of a problem, uncovered through discovery questions, on the customer's entire operation. The objective is to "activate" the customer's interest in solving the problem by helping him or her gain insight into the true ramifications of the problem, and to realize that what may seem to be of little consequence is, in fact, of significant consequence.

PROJECTION QUESTIONS:

Projection questions assist the customer in "projecting" what life would be like without the problems or dissatisfactions uncovered through the activation questions. This helps the customer to see value in finding solutions to the problems developed earlier in the sales call.

TRANSITION QUESTIONS:

Transition questions are simple closed-ended questions that confirm the customer's desire to solve the problem(s) uncovered through the previous questions. These questions make the transition from need confirmation to the sales presentation and lead to commitment.

For a complete discussion of the ADAPT process, see Ingram, T. N., *Certification Study Guide* (The University of Memphis: SMEI Accreditation Institute, 1994).

Harcourt Brace & Company

ADAPT QUESTIONING SCRIPT TEMPLATE

Assessment Questions

SELLER: "Initial area of inquiry—open-ended *assessment* question."
BUYER: "Response to this assessment question."
SELLER: "Follow-up *assessment* question based on above response."
BUYER: "Response to this second assessment question."
SELLER: "Follow-up *assessment* question based on preceding responses."
BUYER: "Response to this third assessment question."

Discovery Questions

SELLER: "Initial *discovery* question based on preceding responses."
BUYER: "Response to this discovery question."
SELLER: "Follow-up *discovery* question based on preceding responses."
BUYER: "Response to this second discovery question."
SELLER: "Follow-up *discovery* question based on preceding responses."
BUYER: "Response to this third discovery question."

Activation Questions

SELLER: "Initial *activation* question based on preceding responses."
BUYER: "Response to this activation question."
SELLER: "Follow-up *activation* question based on preceding responses."
BUYER: "Response to this second activation question."
SELLER: "Follow-up *activation* question based on preceding responses."
BUYER: "Response to this third activation question."

Projection Questions

SELLER: "Initial *projection* question based on preceding responses."
BUYER: "Response to this projection question."
SELLER: "Follow-up *projection* question based on preceding responses."
BUYER: "Response to this second projection question."
SELLER: "Follow-up *projection* question based on preceding responses."
BUYER: "Response to this third projection question."

Transition Questions

SELLER: "Initial *transition* question based on preceding responses."
BUYER: "Response to this transition question."
SELLER: "Follow-up *transition* question based on preceding responses."
BUYER: "Response to this second transition question."
BUYER: "Follow-up *transition* question based on preceding responses."
BUYER: "Response to this third transition question."

Harcourt Brace & Company

Assessment Questions

SELLER:

BUYER:

SELLER:

BUYER:

SELLER:

BUYER:

SELLER:

BUYER:

SELLER:

BUYER:

Discovery Questions

SELLER:

BUYER:

SELLER:

BUYER:

SELLER:

BUYER:

SELLER:

BUYER:

SELLER:

BUYER:

Harcourt Brace & Company

Activation Questions

SELLER:

BUYER:

SELLER:

BUYER:

SELLER:

BUYER:

SELLER:

BUYER:

SELLER:

BUYER:

Projection Questions

SELLER:

BUYER:

SELLER:

BUYER:

SELLER:

BUYER:

SELLER:

BUYER:

SELLER:

BUYER:

Harcourt Brace & Company

Transition Questions

SELLER:

BUYER:

SELLER:

BUYER:

SELLER:

BUYER:

SELLER:

BUYER:

SELLER:

BUYER:

Harcourt Brace & Company

QUESTIONING SKILLS
EXPERIENTIAL EXERCISE 6.4
Activating the ADAPT Process for Developing and Confirming Customer Needs

OBJECTIVE: You will further develop your understanding and ability to apply the ADAPT process of needs development.

THE EXERCISE ASSIGNMENT

Congratulations!! You have recently joined Addvance Frozen Foods as their salesperson in the Midwestern Territory. A food processor specializing in providing the meat entrees for large institutions such as prisons and hospitals, Addvance is recognized as one of the industry leaders. This reputation not only includes market share, but also extends to leadership in innovative products and customer relations.

You have been working for several weeks to gain access to Jane Cummings, the foods buyer for the State of Illinois Prison System. With several other major food processors (including Kraft and General Foods) located in Chicago, the competition in this region has been high. As a result, Addvance has never been able to get any of its product line into the Illinois system. Nevertheless, Addvance has recently introduced and started shipping an innovative turkey-based line of products that averages 18 percent higher protein and 23 percent lower fat content than anything marketed by the competition. The higher protein level per serving is extremely important to such institutions as prisons, as it allows them to meet nutrition requirements with smaller servings of meat entrees and thus creates an opportunity for cost reduction. In addition to these tangible benefits, the product line's average selling price of $2.10 per pound is $0.22 a pound lower than Kraft's competing products and $0.20 under those of General Foods. Documenting the higher protein level and lower fat content certainly got Jane's attention. However, it was the combination of increased protein and lower price that got you the appointment to talk with Jane and members of her buying group in person.

As part of preparing for your sales call, you are compiling a set of anticipated questions that might assist you in better understanding Jane's current situation and confirming her needs. Information gained through this sort of effective questioning has proven valuable to you in the past as it helps you better respond to the customer's needs. Following the ADAPT model of questioning, develop a series of effective Assessment, Discovery, Activation, Projection, and Transition questions that you might use in the sales call with Jane Cummings.

Please use the following workbook pages to develop your questions:

Harcourt Brace & Company

Assessment Questions

1. _____
2. _____
3. _____
4. _____
5. _____
6. _____

Discovery Questions

1. _____
2. _____
3. _____
4. _____
5. _____
6. _____

Activation Questions

1. _____
2. _____
3. _____
4. _____
5. _____
6. _____

Harcourt Brace & Company

Projection Questions

1. _____

2. _____

3. _____

4. _____

5. _____

6. _____

Transition Questions

1. _____

2. _____

3. _____

4. _____

5. _____

6. _____

Harcourt Brace & Company

Harcourt Brace & Company

QUESTIONING SKILLS
EXPERIENTIAL EXERCISE 6.5
Role Plays for *ADAPTive Questioning Part I*

OBJECTIVE: You will continue building your listening skills and self-confidence in ADAPTive questioning through the use of in-class, mini–role plays.

INTRODUCTION

In this role play exercise, the instructor will be the prospect and students will take turns asking each type of question. As the role play progresses, it should become easier for you to understand the ADAPT process and what is required to make it effective.

THE COMPANY YOU REPRESENT

Students assume the role of salesperson for Sonoco. Founded in 1899 as the Southern Novelty Company, Sonoco Products Corporation is headquartered in Hartsville, South Carolina. This past year, it employed 17,000 people in 24 countries and ranked 22nd on the *Fortune* 500 list. For that same year, the company earned $117.5 million on nearly $2 billion in sales. The company specializes in producing many different types of packaging, from composite cans that hold orange juice, noodles, and tennis balls to labels that cover dozens of products in the health care and medical industry. Textile companies worldwide use the company's paper and plastic cones and tubes. The company also produces industrial containers, caulking tubes, recyclable plastic grocery bags, and even paper lids on the glasses travelers find at hotels.

YOUR PRODUCT

Sonoco produces both chipboard and corrugated partitions that are custom designed to fit the customer's packaging needs. The partitions are designed so that all cells within the box have the same size, which means that the product fits snugly throughout the box, minimizing chances for breakage and scratching. The company also manufactures machinery for inserting products into boxes. The following chart summarizes the features and advantages of Sonoco's packaging products:

FEATURE	ADVANTAGE
Custom designed and manufactured	Packaging will fit snugly around any size or shape product
Broad range of surface finishes, including water and starch finished, wax impregnated, and polyethylene coated	Allows versatility in shipping; not necessary to shop from several manufacturers to meet different packaging requirements
Automatic product insertion machinery available	Provides smooth product insertion without damage to glass or labeling
Easy-grip edges	Keeps partitions from falling out of cartons during manual or automatic decasing
Uses recyclable cardboard	Meets demand for environmental awareness
Durable, solid fibers	Helps withstand abrupt shocks
Clean, uniform edges and surfaces	Product arrives clean, dustfree, and looking its best
Custom-designed graphics available for outside of package	Can enhance company image and make product easier to sell in self-service stores
Frequent delivery available	Reduces need for large inventory of empty packaging
Design of flutes provides stronger boxes with less weight	Provides maximum protection while reducing shipping costs

THE EXERCISE ASSIGNMENT

In this role play, it is assumed that the Lily Fields Glass Co. has called Sonoco and expressed an interest in Sonoco's packaging. This lead has been turned over to you, and today you will make the initial call on the purchasing manager of the Lilly Fields Glass Co., a manufacturer of water glasses, water pitchers, cocktail glasses, and glass beer steins. Its products are all currently sold to bars and restaurants.

Your task in this call is to first use **Assessment** questions to find out more about the Lilly Fields Glass Co. For example, are they considering any changes in their target market? Then, using **Discovery** questions, **Activation** questions, **Projection** questions, and **Transition** questions, explore (a) the prospect's problems; (b) the consequences of these problems; and (c) what solving these problems might mean to the purchasing manager. However, *you will not present solutions during this role play.*

Harcourt Brace & Company

To assist you in preparing for this call, here are examples of the kinds of problems your prospect might be having:

- Lilly Fields may need equipment to automatically insert glass products into shipping containers.
- Lilly Fields may need packaging with nonstandard specifications.
- Lilly Fields may need different materials incorporated into the same package.
- Lilly Fields may not know how to go about designing packaging.
- Lilly Fields may have been having a lot of damage in shipping.
- Lilly Fields may be spending a lot for extra warehouse space to store packaging.
- The purchasing manager may also have personal needs beyond those of the firm.

Based on the features and advantages explained earlier, you should be able to think of other problems that might be solved by using your product.

Prepare for the call by listing the potential consequences you might want to explore during the call. Use the **Salesperson's Preparation Form** provided for your use on the following pages to list questions you could use during the role play. A few possible questions have been provided to get you started. At this point, don't be too concerned about the quality of the questions; it is more important that you focus on getting practice asking each kind of question. As you go through the next several role plays, you will learn more about what provides quality to each kind of question.

Remember that the purpose of the role play is to practice ADAPT questioning. Do not "pitch" to the prospect. Focus instead on getting information about his or her problems, needs, and concerns.

You will also be asked to summarize what you have heard and check that the prospect agrees with your summary. If you were going to propose a solution, you would want to be certain that you had properly interpreted the prospect's concerns.

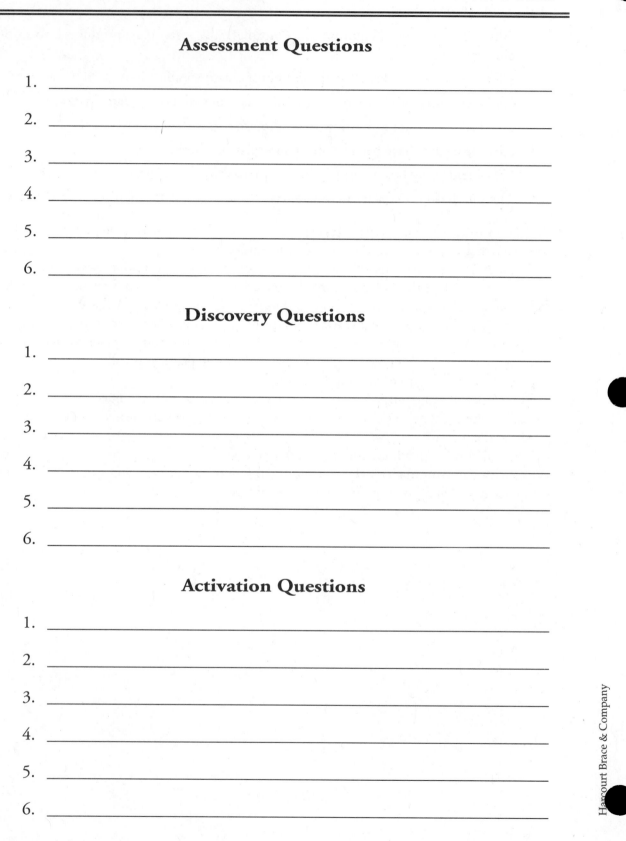

SALESPERSON'S PREPARATION FORM

Assessment Questions

1. _____
2. _____
3. _____
4. _____
5. _____
6. _____

Discovery Questions

1. _____
2. _____
3. _____
4. _____
5. _____
6. _____

Activation Questions

1. _____
2. _____
3. _____
4. _____
5. _____
6. _____

Harcourt Brace & Company

Projection Questions

1. _____
2. _____
3. _____
4. _____
5. _____
6. _____

Transition Questions

1. _____
2. _____
3. _____
4. _____
5. _____
6. _____

Harcourt Brace & Company

◉

QUESTIONING SKILLS
EXPERIENTIAL EXERCISE 6.6
*Role Plays for **ADAPT**ive Questioning Part II*

✳

OBJECTIVE: You will continue building your listening skills and self-confidence in using ADAPTive questioning through in-class, mini–role plays.

THE EXERCISE ASSIGNMENT

This role play will provide you with additional opportunities and experience working with the ADAPT questioning sequence. The class will be divided into groups of three and the role play divided into three rounds so that you will have an opportunity to play a salesperson, a prospect, and an observer. You are not expected to "act" during these role plays. Rather, your focus should be on practicing the listening and questioning skills.

SALESPERSON INSTRUCTIONS

Use the completed Salesperson's Preparation (ADAPT questions) Form you prepared for the preceding exercise but during the role play, try to be ready to respond to what the prospect says rather than sticking to your exact prepared questions. Paraphrase—your questions should reflect and build from what your prospect says in responding to prior questions.

In this role play, it is assumed that Chateau Memphis, a small vintner quickly gaining acclaim for its fine table wines, has called Sonoco and expressed an interest in packaging. This lead has now been turned over to you, and today you will make the initial call on the winery manager. The image of Chateau Memphis is one of quality and reliability and its customers are small retailers and restaurants in the southern United States.

PROSPECT INFORMATION

As the prospect, you will play the part of the manager at Chateau Memphis. During the role play, you should respond to the salesperson in a natural manner. Be cooperative and answer the questions that you are asked. *Do not* ask the salesperson specific or detailed questions about the features of Sonoco's packaging. Remember, the purpose of this exercise

Harcourt Brace & Company

is to give the salesperson a chance to use his or her questioning skills to reach an under-standing of your needs. In preparation for playing the buyer's role, consider the answers you will give if asked questions similar to the following:

- How are purchasing decisions made here?
- How many employees do you have?
- What brand of equipment do you use now?
- How many people use it?
- How many retailers/restaurants do you supply?
- How much warehouse space do you have? What percent is being used?
- What are the steps your company currently uses to design packaging for shipments?

OBSERVER INSTRUCTIONS

You are the observer for this round of role play. Observe what happens. Pay special atten-tion to:

- the listening skills demonstrated by the salesperson.
- inquiries about the prospect's situation.
- the exploration of problems the prospect is having.
- questions about consequences linked to the problems.
- questions about benefits to be derived from resolving the needs that have been dis-covered.
- whether there is an accurate summary of the needs discovered during the meeting.

Record your observations on the **Observation Form** provided in the following pages of your experiential workbook. Review the sample form before coming to class so that you will know how to use the blank form as you watch the role play develop. When the role play has concluded, briefly review your observations with both the salesperson and prospect. Invite the person who played the prospect to participate in the discussion.

Harcourt Brace & Company

Your Name: _____

SAMPLE OBSERVATION FORM

Prospect's Name: _____ Salesperson's Name: _____

	I PARTICULARLY LIKED . . .	YOU MIGHT FIND IT HELPFUL TO . . .
PRELIMINARIES:		
Stated prospect name, own name, company name		*Didn't state own name*
Stated reason for call	*Established purpose of visit and sounded friendly*	
Stated anticipated length of call		
Explained approach to doing business		*Check if prospect is interested in continuing*
Transition to Investigating		
QUESTIONING:		
Assessment Questions	*Made buyer feel you were interested*	*How long has buyer been there? Who is current supplier?*
Discovery Questions		*No matter what was said, you'd reply "OK" and go to the next question. Your questions should follow from buyer's responses.*
Activation Questions	*Established implications of increasing costs*	*Did not establish implications of the packaging falling apart when it gets wet.*
Projection Questions		*What will elimination of problems mean to buyer? To company?*
Transition Questions	*Nice job of confirming prospect's desire to solve the cost problem*	*Left the wet packaging problem untouched.*
SUMMARY OF NEEDS DISCOVERED:		*Only mentioned problems, didn't show needs.*
COMMUNICATION SKILLS:		
Encouraging Statements	*"I'm glad you asked that question"*	
Clarifying Information		
Conversational Tone		
Nonverbal Communication	*Natural hand gestures*	*Drumming pencil on table is distracting*

Harcourt Brace & Company

Your Name: _____

OBSERVATION FORM

Prospect's Name: _____   Salesperson's Name: _____

	I PARTICULARLY LIKED . . .	YOU MIGHT FIND IT HELPFUL TO . . .

PRELIMINARIES:

Stated prospect name, own name, company name

Stated reason for call

Stated anticipated length of call

Explained approach to doing business

Transition to Investigating

QUESTIONING:

Assessment Questions

Discovery Questions

Activation Questions

Projection Questions

Transition Questions

SUMMARY OF NEEDS DISCOVERED:

COMMUNICATION SKILLS:

Encouraging Statements

Clarifying Information

Conversational Tone

Nonverbal Communication

Harcourt Brace & Company

MODULE SEVEN

LISTENING SKILLS

The importance of listening in professional selling cannot be over-emphasized. It is virtually impossible for salespeople to achieve credibility in the eyes of the buyer without listening to the buyer's point of view. And, without credibility, very few sales will be made. Even so, listening has been an overlooked topic in most sales training programs until recent years. Although communication skills have been included in most programs, emphasis has typically been given to verbal sales techniques, and occasionally the development of written sales proposals. Even today, most salespeople have received very little, if any, formal training in listening.

In more progressive sales organizations, however, listening is becoming a key topic in sales training. Sales trainers further indicate that listening has become an extremely important training topic. Whether or not they have received training in listening, today's successful sales professional exhibits strong listening skills that benefit both the buyer and the seller.

Listening is essential for trust-based relationship selling. How can a salesperson demonstrate a true **customer orientation** and understand customer needs without listening? How can salespeople be **dependable** unless they carefully listen and properly interpret customer requests? Certainly, good listening is common courtesy and makes the salesperson more **likable,** but listening also helps make efficient use of the buyer's time. There is no doubt that in today's selling environment, listening is a critical element of salespeoples' **competence** in most aspects of trust-based relationship selling.

Professional salespeople are willing to do more than merely listen to the prospect's point of view. They combine questioning and listening skills to gain in-depth knowledge of the buyer's needs, constraints, preferences, personality, and communication styles.

There are some difficulties in listening that salespeople can overcome. The two most common errors made by salespeople are talking too much and paying too little attention to what the customer is saying, Because salespeople are experts on their products and services, they are comfortable and feel "in control" while talking. This causes some salespeople to talk too much in proportion to how much the customer is talking. It is important

Harcourt Brace & Company

to remember that the customer is always interested in what he or she is saying, but not always interested in what the salesperson is saying. By listening carefully to the customer, salespeople increase the odds of responding in an interesting, informative, and timely manner. There is also a tendency to think that we can do other things (such as calculate prices, think about what to say next, and so on) while listening. In most cases, we are overestimating our mind's ability to process multiple thoughts simultaneously, and the buyer will easily detect that the salesperson is preoccupied or distracted.

To become better listeners, salespeople must make a commitment to concentrate during all conversations with customers. They must see the value in listening and have a strong motivation to listen. The exercises in this module help develop an awareness of the importance of listening and provide several opportunities to sharpen your listening skills. Experiential Exercise 7.1 (*Your Listening Habits: A Self-Assessment*) asks you to honestly evaluate your own listening behaviors. To improve any behavior, it is a good idea to "take inventory" of your current behavior so you can identify specific areas for improvement. It might also be fun to have a close friend or family member rate your listening skills on the same dimensions shown in Exercise 7.1.

Experiential Exercise 7.2 (*The Importance of Being a Good Listener*) reinforces the crucial role of listening in professional selling and asks you to target specific skills, people, and situations for enhancing your listening performance. You can learn a lot about listening by identifying good and bad listeners among those you interact with on a regular basis. More than coincidence, those you identify as good listeners in Exercise 7.2 would probably rate high on your list of good conversationalists.

In Exercise 7.3 (*Concentration: Getting Beyond the Background Interference and Noise*), you move directly into the sales context as you learn about Jim Jones, the purchasing agent for LB & M Bearing Corporation. In this exercise, you and your classmates will recall individual perceptions about a sales scenario. These perceptions will be compared and contrasted as a means of reminding us that we must get past distractions to become effective listeners. Exercise 7.4 (*Experiencing Active versus Reactive Listening*) illustrates the mental challenge of dealing with more complex verbal messages. In all likelihood, you will make more mistakes as you attempt **reactive** listening than when only **active** listening is required. In professional selling, messages from buyers are often complex, and signals are sometimes confusing. Thus, sharpening your mind can help improve listening and sales performance.

The last two exercises in this module provide opportunities for you to demonstrate the ability to concentrate on a spoken message and recall basic facts. Exercise 7.5 (*Narration of the Battle of the Little Big Horn*) details some little-known aspects of the famous encounter in which General Custer's unit was annihilated. Exercise 7.6 (*A Listening Test*) will remind many of your classmates (hopefully not you) of the difficulty of listening, even for a couple of minutes.

◎

LISTENING SKILLS
EXPERIENTIAL EXERCISE 7.1
Your Listening Habits: A Self-Assessment

OBJECTIVE: You will assess your listening habits and have a better understanding of critical listening behaviors.

THE EXERCISE ASSIGNMENT

Listening skill development is an ongoing process. Good listening is a key to success in any business environment. Discovering your attitude about listening is an important first step toward successful listening. Attitudes determine our behaviors. To discover your listening attitudes, complete the following exercise. If a statement describes your listening attitude or behavior check "Yes," if not, check "No." Be toughminded.

Listening Attitudes and Behaviors

	YES	NO
1. I am interested in many subjects and do not knowingly tune out dry-sounding information.	❏	❏
2. I listen carefully for a speaker's main ideas and supporting points.	❏	❏
3. I take notes during meetings to record key points.	❏	❏
4. I am not easily distracted.	❏	❏
5. I keep my emotions under control.	❏	❏
6. I concentrate carefully and do not fake attention.	❏	❏
7. I wait for the speaker to finish before finally evaluating the message.	❏	❏
8. I respond appropriately with a smile, a nod, or a word of acknowledgment, as a speaker is talking.	❏	❏
9. I am aware of mannerisms that may distract a speaker and keep mine under control.	❏	❏

Harcourt Brace & Company

		YES	NO
10.	I understand my biases and control them when I am listening.	❏	❏
11	I refrain from constantly interrupting.	❏	❏
12.	I value eye contact and maintain it most of the time.	❏	❏
13.	I often restate or paraphrase what the speaker said to make sure I have the correct meaning.	❏	❏
14.	I listen for the speaker's emotional meaning as well as subject matter content.	❏	❏
15.	I ask questions for clarification.	❏	❏
16.	I do not finish other people's sentences unless asked to do so.	❏	❏
17.	When listening on the telephone one hand is kept free to take notes.	❏	❏
18.	I attempt to set aside my ego and focus on the speaker rather than on myself.	❏	❏
19.	I am careful to judge the message rather than the speaker.	❏	❏
20.	I am a patient listener most of the time.	❏	❏

The following scale will help you interpret your present listening skill level based on your current attitudes and behaviors.

1–5 "No" answers	You are an excellent listener. Keep it up!
6–10 "No" answers	You are a good listener, but can improve.
11–15 "No" answers	Through practice you can become a much more effective listener in your business and personal relationships.
16–20 "No" answers	Listen up!

Source: Bone, Diane. *The Business of Listening: A Practical Guide to Effective Listening* (Crisp Publications, 1988), p. 30–31.

Harcourt Brace & Company

LISTENING SKILLS
EXPERIENTIAL EXERCISE 7.2
The Importance of Being a Good Listener

OBJECTIVE: You will evaluate the listening behavior of both a good and poor listener with which you have been in contact. From this evaluation you will better understand the importance of being a good listener while developing and targeting areas of your listening behavior upon which you can improve.

THE EXERCISE ASSIGNMENT

It is important to know how well you understand and remember what you hear. All of us can profit by listening more closely. A well-trained pair of ears is one of our most valuable assets, and here's why. Experts estimate that most of us spend about 70 percent of our waking hours in some form of verbal communication. Specifically:

  9 percent of our time is spent writing.
 16 percent is spent reading.
 30 percent is devoted to talking.
 45 percent of the time, almost half the time we are awake, is spent listening.

THE IMPORTANCE OF BEING A GOOD LISTENER

We listen more than we do any other activity except breathe!

Listening is:

- the weakest link in our communication system.
- the result of bad habits that develop because we haven't been trained to listen effectively.
- a skill that can be learned.
- a prime tool of the salesperson.
- an essential ingredient for leadership.
- a matter of desire and concentration.

Harcourt Brace & Company

Please respond to the following statements:

1. Think of the best listener you know. List this person's listening behaviors.

2. Think of the worst listener you know. List this person's listening behaviors.

3. Based on the listening skills of the worst listener you know, some of the listening behaviors you want to improve on are:

4. I will consciously use more effective listening behaviors

    a. in the following situations:

    b. when interacting with the following people:

Harcourt Brace & Company

LISTENING SKILLS
EXPERIENTIAL EXERCISE 7.3
Concentration—Getting Beyond The Background Interference And Noise

OBJECTIVE: You will become aware of Active and Reactive listening. You will be better able to concentrate and remember what you hear. In addition, you will be able to distinguish and comprehend facts within a conversation. Active and Reactive listening do not just happen—they are skills that are learned and developed through use.

INTRODUCTION

At the beginning of a class period, your instructor or facilitator will ask you to turn to the corresponding worksheet in your student workbooks, put down your pencils or pens, and just listen. The instructor will then read a short selling scenario aloud. The scenario describes a selling situation and gives 14 specific facts that would be important to the salesperson calling on this account. These facts center around the existing buyer–seller relationship; the nature of the buying task; and certain problems, needs, and wants of the buyer.

After hearing the scenario, record as many facts as you can recall in the proper location on the worksheet.

Discuss your results with your classmates. Who remembered how many? What did those who remembered a high number do that differed from those who scored low? What can we do as participants in a conversation to select out spurious background noise and improve our listening concentration?

Harcourt Brace & Company

THE EXERCISE ASSIGNMENT

Based on the selling scenario that your instructor has just completed reading, record your answers to the following:

What is the nature of the current relationship between the buyer and seller?

1. _____

2. _____

3. _____

4. _____

What characteristics have changed regarding the buyer's current situation?

1. _____

2. _____

3. _____

4. _____

What buyer problems or needs are evident?

1. _____

2. _____

3. _____

4. _____

5. _____

6. _____

Harcourt Brace & Company

◉

LISTENING SKILLS
EXPERIENTIAL EXERCISE 7.4
Experiencing Active versus Reactive Listening

OBJECTIVE: You will understand the different levels of cognition required in Active as opposed to Reactive listening.

INTRODUCTION

Turn to the response page in your workbook that corresponds to this exercise. Put your pencil or pen down. Your instructor will read a series of number sequence challenges. Each number sequence challenge asks you to perform a specific action. After your instructor reads each number sequence challenge, pick up your pen or pencil and write the answer on your worksheet. Put your pen or pencil down and listen to the next challenge.

After you have completed all ten challenges, discuss the results with your classmates. Was there any difference in the type of concentration and comprehension required from one sequence challenge to another? Consider the nature of the cognitive tasks required by each challenge.

In most classes, as the level of cognitive involvement increases, the number of correct scores decreases. This simple exercise offers a good illustration of what the term **reactive listening** means. How can you use this type of listening in a selling situation dealing with facts and statements offered by the customer to which you must respond?

THE EXERCISE ASSIGNMENT

After your instructor reads each number sequence challenge, record your answer on the following lines.

1. _____

2. _____

3. _____

4. _____

5. _____

6. _____

7. _____

8. _____

9. _____

10. _____

Total Number Correct: _____

What differences did you notice in the type of concentration and comprehension required from one sequence challenge to another?

_____

_____

_____

_____

_____

_____

_____

Adapted from "Now Hear This! Teaching Your Students Listening Skills," *Learning 94*.

Harcourt Brace & Company

◉

LISTENING SKILLS
EXPERIENTIAL EXERCISE 7.5
Narration of the Battle of the Little Big Horn   ✳

OBJECTIVE: You will be able to demonstrate the difficulty in listening to and comprehending a message.

THE EXERCISE ASSIGNMENT

In this exercise, a member of the class will read a short narrative aloud. After you have
listened to the story, you will be asked to answer 10 questions, which will be read by
your instructor. Record your response to each of these questions on the corresponding
line below.

1. _____
2. _____
3. _____
4. _____
5. _____
6. _____
7. _____
8. _____
9. _____
10. _____

LISTENING SKILLS
EXPERIENTIAL EXERCISE 7.6
A Listening Test

OBJECTIVE: You will be able to demonstrate the difficulty in listening to and comprehending a message.

THE EXERCISE ASSIGNMENT

In this exercise, a member of the class will read a short narrative aloud. After you have listened to the story, you will be asked to answer 10 questions, which will be read by your instructor. Record your response to each of these questions on the corresponding line below.

1. _____

2. _____

3. _____

4. _____

5. _____

6. _____

7. _____

8. _____

9. _____

10. _____

MODULE EIGHT

WRITTEN COMMUNICATION SKILLS

Those who lack experience in selling view it primarily as a verbal process rather than as a comprehensive communication process. As you have learned in previous modules, professional selling requires that salespeople be well-rounded communicators, skilled in questioning, listening, and presenting information. Verbal communication is extremely important to most salespeople, but written communication is also vitally important.

With multimedia sales presentations becoming more routine, you might think that written sales communication would be declining in importance. Actually, the opposite is true. With the widespread use of multimedia, the standards for all sales communication continues to rise. Buyers expect clear, informative sales messages and they are less tolerant of sloppy communication. Because everyone knows that most word processing programs have sub-routines to check spelling and grammar, for example, mistakes are less acceptable.

There are several situations in which written sales communication is especially important. In sales of major magnitude, effective written communication becomes critical. Contracts, written sales proposals, and letters often document the entire process and agreement between parties. Many purchasing decisions involve multiple influences, as described in Module Three. In such situations, written communication can keep all parties informed simultaneously. Further, multi-part sales messages such as detailed sales proposals can be dissected and evaluated by the appropriate people in the buying center. Written communication is often essential in sales to customers across national boundaries. Another situation in which written communication can be crucial is when legal issues are relevant, including the granting of promises or implied warranties. And, on an everyday basis, salespeople rely on written communication as another means of staying in touch with customers.

Since written communication provides a permanent record of claims and intentions, salespeople should be careful not to overpromise while still maintaining a positive tone. No buyer wants to read a proposal full of legal disclaimers and warnings, yet such information may be a necessary ingredient in certain written communication. As with all communication, salespeople should try to give buyers the information they need to make informed decisions.

Harcourt Brace & Company

Written communication offers salespeople a real opportunity to differentiate themselves from their competitors. Recent college graduates are similar to business people in general in that their verbal communications skills often exceed their written communications skills. Those who work on written communications skills usually stand out from the crowd, and they do not spend as much time laboring to achieve effectiveness in their written communication. In this module, you have the opportunity to improve in an area where almost everyone could benefit from improvement, and you will also gain from learning more about your own attributes as a job candidate.

Experiential Exercise 8.1 (*Cover Letter of Introduction*) involves writing an error-free letter introducing your college or university to a business person. The letter will include a discussion of some of the products and benefits available from your school. In Experiential Exercise 8.2 (*Written Sales Proposals—Summarizing Quantitative Data*), you will bring quantitative data to life as part of a sales proposal. Facts and Figures can be boring, but when properly presented, they motivate the buyer to take action. You will also develop a cover letter in this exercise.

The next three exercises allow you to learn more about written sales communication by thinking of yourself as a job candidate. Your job is to sell yourself to a prospective employer. Experiential Exercise 8.3 (*Resume Writing I: Identifying Your Accomplishments and Skills*) takes you through an extensive self-analysis resulting in a listing of twelve skills and accomplishments relevant to the job market. After reflecting on this list, you will rank the skills and accomplishments in the order of importance to the job market. From here, you will move on to the next step in the job search in Experiential Exercise 8.4 (*Resume Writing II: Preparing Your Resume*). This exercise gives you practical insights and a recommended format for writing an accomplishments-oriented resume. In Experiential Exercise 8.5 (*Resume Writing III: Developing a Marketing Letter*), you learn about cover letters in the sales process. In this exercise, you will see how cover letters are used for different purposes, and you will learn about different strategies to maximize the effectiveness of cover letters.

WRITTEN COMMUNICATION SKILLS
EXPERIENTIAL EXERCISE 8.1
Cover Letter of Introduction

OBJECTIVE: You will be able to write a letter of introduction.

THE EXERCISE ASSIGNMENT

Corporate America has been critical of business students because of their lack of writing skills. This exercise will allow you to be creative in writing a letter of introduction to a prospective business, introducing your school.

Your letter should include:

1. Your name

2. The name of the school you attend

3. Products of the school (that is, degree programs and students)

4. Benefits the business might be interested in (for example, becoming involved with the school through internships, practicums, and potential student employees)

Harcourt Brace & Company

WRITTEN COMMUNICATION SKILLS
EXPERIENTIAL EXERCISE 8.2
Written Sales Proposals—
Summarizing Quantitative Data

OBJECTIVE: You will be able to present numbers and related data in clear, summarized formats for maximum clarity and persuasive impact.

INTRODUCTION

In this exercise, you will work in groups of two or three to develop a written sales proposal including quantitative product costs and client benefits, a clear synopsis of a timetable for installation, and a summary of the terms of a contract. This proposal has been requested by the client following four sales calls in which needs and expectations have been fully explored. The formal written proposal is to be mailed to the client along with a cover letter.

THE EXERCISE ASSIGNMENT

You are a salesperson for PRE-SELECT, Inc. (PSI). Headquartered in Chicago, PSI is the industry leader in pre-interview assessment and testing for the insurance industry. Focusing primarily on sales-related recruiting and selection, PSI's Interactive Employee Assessment System (IEAS) has been quite successful in lowering payroll costs by reducing sales agent turnover rates. Because of its highly recognized rate of success, PSI's customers include 13 of the top 20 insurance companies in the United States.

Although the system is continuously revised and updated, the basic program has been operating for six years. Using a personal computer in the field—usually at the branch office or agent's location—the IEAS consists of three computer-based components:

1. Pre-interview attitude and aptitude testing
2. Interactive simulations of critical work situations for use as part of the interview process
3. Periodic, post-hiring assessment for training focus

Salesperson Instructions

Ron Lovell, National Agency Director for Secure Future Insurance Company (SFIC), is interested in improving his company's recruiting and selection process for sales agents. SFIC is a national company with 150 agents across the United States. Although not ranked among the top 20 insurers, SFIC is a large and successful firm listed in the *Fortune* 1000. You have met with Ron on four previous occasions exploring problems, opportunities, and needs. During these meetings you discovered that SFIC's turnover rate among its sales agents approaches 42 percent. Compared to industry averages, that's not bad, but it does require hiring 375 new salespeople every year. SFIC's own estimate of hiring, training, and licensing costs is $7,500, for a total annual cost exceeding $2.8 million. Field experience indicates that, using PSI's computer-based system, turnover would fall to an average ranging from 15 to 20 percent, which offers considerable savings to SFIC.

You have been working up the figures for implementing the system at headquarters and in each of the 150 general offices. One-time hardware costs total $610,000. Although minimal training is required, installation and training would be priced out at $75,000 plus another $5,500 for chargeable travel expenses. Software licensing fees would total $135,000 per year. Sales tax on the hardware and software license would be computed at 6.5 percent. Finally, software maintenance fees run 15 percent of the annual licensing cost. According to the technical support department, this installation could be completed, with the full system operating in just over 4 months from the date of the order.

During your last call, you detailed the basics of the Interactive Employee Assessment System scaled to meet the needs of SFIC. Ron, along with the other officers attending the presentation, liked what he saw and requested that you put together a formal proposal. On your way out of the building, Ron mentioned that the proposal would have to be detailed enough to allow him to pass it through the capital budgeting department. This means detailing costs, projected savings, the payback period, and the installation-implementation schedule. As another positive indicator, Ron also asked that you arrange a follow-up meeting approximately 2 weeks after the proposal is received. Your task is to develop a follow-up letter and written sales proposal for his immediate attention.

Harcourt Brace & Company

WRITTEN COMMUNICATION SKILLS
EXPERIENTIAL EXERCISE 8.3
Resume Writing I:
Identifying Your Accomplishments and Skills

OBJECTIVE: You will increase your understanding of the resume process while developing your own resume in preparation for graduation.

IDENTIFYING MEANINGFUL
ACCOMPLISHMENTS AND SKILLS

The Foundation for Your Job Search

An effective self-analysis provides the foundation for your job search campaign. It directs you by identifying what you have to "sell." If you can think of yourself as "being on the market," then your first need is to define clearly what your product qualities are, or the skills and strengths that you have to offer in the job market.

To describe your qualities, you need to go beyond the title or task description of your last job and become aware of your general experience, background, knowledge, skills, and abilities. You should be able to break down your jobs into their component parts. This preciseness will help you visualize and plan how those very same strengths might be *transferable* to a new type of job that, on the surface, appears to be quite different from your recent work.

Accomplishments

As you look back over your last few years on the job or in school, you can recollect special things you have done that made you very proud. These were the times when you went beyond the call of duty—meeting an emergency, solving a problem, or seizing a red-hot opportunity. Usually these accomplishments were of great benefit to your employer, to your fellow workers, to your peers in school, or to yourself. The accomplishment may or may not have received recognition or praise from someone higher up. More important, these achievements illustrate your skills and capabilities—your future potential for solving problems.

THE EXERCISE ASSIGNMENT

Your first assignment is to discover and write down 12 lifetime accomplishments. Aim for completeness rather than conciseness. You may discover that you have a lot more to be proud of than you thought. However, the purpose in writing the accomplishments is not merely to boost your self-esteem (although that is a worthwhile by-product). Writing down your accomplishments will:

Harcourt Brace & Company

- supply you with material for creating or enhancing your resume.

- give you a foundation for deriving your skills and strengths.

- make you more comfortable about recounting your strengths—in a letter or in an interview.

To get started writing your first accomplishments:

- Identify a problem, opportunity, or situation you faced at work or at school that required you to take some sort of action.

- Explain the action or approach that you took in solving the problem or taking advantage of the opportunity. Your explanation should focus on how you analyzed and prepared to solve the problem and on the resources (people, equipment, and so on) you used in your solution or plan.

- Identify the results you obtained. Results may be quantified in terms of savings, days, sales volume, and so on or qualified in terms of usefulness to yourself or others. Or you might explain how the plan was implemented and who utilized the information.

Where to Look

In digging up your accomplishments, don't feel obliged to look for something cosmic. Some of your accomplishments may be so noteworthy that you will want to use them later in your resume or in an interview. But other, less spectacular accomplishments may be equally useful in uncovering your true talents, skills, knowledge, and strengths. In fact, you may find key accomplishments performed off the job. For example, you may have accomplished great things in community activities or in your church; if so, do not hesitate to list these as valid accomplishments. Accomplishments in school are valid indicators of what you have to "sell." Remember, an accomplishment is not dictated by the rewards you receive from the outside world, but by your own sense of satisfaction for having done the job.

Use the following to "jog your memory":

- Did you take the initiative to solve a problem or address an issue that no one else was tackling?

- Did you see an opportunity for great improvement, develop a plan to seize the opportunity, and help carry it through to success?

- Did you develop a new gadget or new approach that improved daily output?

- Did you conceive of or create a new organization, function, service, department, or product that filled an important niche?

- Did you devise and carry through a complex plan or procedure, perhaps for the first time?

- Did you participate with your peers or superiors at work or school on an important project where your input was part of the key to its success?

- Have you dealt with customers? Were some of them irate? How did you deal with them? What skills did you use in this type of situation?

Harcourt Brace & Company

- Did you have responsibility for scheduling employees for work or an ongoing project that needed to be completed on a timely basis?
- Were you ever left to supervise yourself and/or others? What kinds of things were you responsible for?
- Did you support yourself while you were in school?
- Did you "close" at your place of work?
- Were you involved in clubs at school? Were you an officer? Did you start or help start any new activities? Have you been in charge of any projects?
- Do you have any specific computer hardware or software knowledge?
- Did you complete any major projects in classes that relate to your desired job?
- Did you ever train other employees?
- Were you ever in charge of inventory or buying for inventory?
- Do you have any academic honors?
- Did you participate in an internship program?

How You Say It Is Important Too!!

When writing your accomplishments, *begin by using action words* where possible. Examples of these clear-cut, punchy words follow:

Action Words

Administer	Communicate	Direct	Handle
Advise	Compare	Distribute	Identify
Affect	Conceive	Draft	Implement
Analyze	Conceptualize	Edit	Improve
Anticipate	Consult	Educate	Increase
Apply	Contract	Encourage	Influence
Approach	Control	Enlarge	Inform
Approve	Cooperate	Enlist	Initiate
Arrange	Coordinate	Establish	Innovate
Assemble	Counsel	Estimate	Install
Assess	Create	Evaluate	Institute
Assign	Decide	Examine	Instruct
Assist	Define	Execute	Integrate
Attain	Delegate	Expand	Investigate
Author	Demonstrate	Expedite	Invent
Build	Design	Facilitate	Lead
Calculate	Detail	Forecast	Maintain
Catalog	Determine	Formulate	Manage
Chair	Develop	Generate	Manipulate
Collaborate	Devise	Guide	Market

Harcourt Brace & Company

Mediate	Prepare	Report	Successful
Merchandise	Present	Represent	Summarize
Moderate	Preside	Reorganize	Supervise
Modify	Problem-solve	Research	Support
Monitor	Process	Resolve	Survey
Motivate	Produce	Responsible	Synthesize
Negotiate	Promote	Review	Systemize
Obtain	Provide	Revise	Teach
Operate	Recommend	Scan	Team
Order	Reconcile	Schedule	Team-build
Organize	Record	Screen	Technical
Originate	Recruit	Select	Train
Participate	Rectify	Serve	Transmit
Perform	Re-design	Speak	Update
Persuade	Reduce	Staff	Utilize
Placate	Relate	Standardize	Versatile
Plan	Renew	Simulate	Write

Resumes should clearly accent those accomplishments that transfer as work related skills. How you phrase these is also important. Translate accomplishments so they represent benefits to your target companies. Sample accomplishments follow. Notice that several of these accomplishments are quantified as to *results*. When the accomplishments are used in your resume, they should be condensed (usually to two or three lines) without losing their impact.

Work Related Accomplishments

- Managed warehouse and accounted for $300,000 inventory.
- Received *Salesperson of the Month* Award 4 times.
- Achieved 2nd Place in *Salesperson of the Year* Competition.
- Averaged 137 percent of quota over 3 years.

Career Related Achievements

- National Sales Hall of Fame Winner—4th out of 200 salespeople.
- Headed Marketing Committee for Pi Sigma Epsilon, a Professional Fraternity in Sales and Marketing.
- Headed Student Program at Illinois Central College.
- Organized and Directed the 1995 *Illinois State University Follies.*

Now, think what you have been doing over the past 3 or 4 years. What are your accomplishments and achievements? How are they career related? After you have identified and recalled 12 accomplishments, write them out in the space provided. Don't forget to use the action verbs that were listed earlier. After you have filled in all 12 accomplishments, compare them and rank each one in describing your value in the job market. You may decide to use the top-ranked ones to produce an accomplishment-oriented resume, rather than a list of job descriptions.

Harcourt Brace & Company

Name: _____

My Accomplishments and Achievements

DESCRIPTION OF ACCOMPLISHMENT	RANK
• _____	
_____	_____
• _____	
_____	_____
• _____	
_____	_____
• _____	
_____	_____
• _____	
_____	_____
• _____	
_____	_____
• _____	
_____	_____
• _____	
_____	_____
• _____	
_____	_____
• _____	
_____	_____

Harcourt Brace & Company

WRITTEN COMMUNICATION SKILLS
EXPERIENTIAL EXERCISE 8.4
Resume Writing II:
Preparing Your Resume

OBJECTIVE: You will develop your own resume in preparation for graduation.

PREPARING YOUR RESUME

Purposes of a Resume

To prepare the most effective resume, you need to consider your target employer. An ideal resume will reveal your most saleable skills and attributes as they relate to a specific position within a certain company. The resume should be designed to *arouse* a prospective employer's interest and *inspire* the employer to call you for an interview. The resume should provide enough information to show the employer that you are qualified for the job, but at the same time create compelling questions in the mind of the recruiter.

This means you *should not* tell the employer "everything there is to know" about yourself. If you provide too much detail, a recruiter might notice an item that excludes you, or the recruiter might not be inspired to find out more about you.

To arouse interest, a resume should be like a good advertisement—a deliberately crafted picture that beckons the reader to learn more through personal contact. Rather than tell all, you tell what is interesting and relevant for the reader's needs.

Different Resume Formats

The two most commonly used formats are *chronological* and *functional*.

- The *chronological resume* emphasizes your employment record—your job titles, where you worked, how long, and what responsibilities you held. Your jobs are listed in reverse order, beginning with the most recent.

- The *functional resume* emphasizes the kinds of work you have done and what you accomplished in various aspects of business.

Actually, each type incorporates a bit of the other. The chronological resume becomes more meaningful when you list accomplishments under each job. Likewise, a functional resume will usually have a condensed employment history (showing company, date, and job title).

Harcourt Brace & Company

The functional resume organizes work experience by functions, such as general marketing, management, production, finance, or any of their subfunctions. It usually incorporates a range of accomplishments to illustrate the job seeker's expertise in each area.

In addition to these two main types of resume, others exist to fit special situations. For example, in the academic world the emphasis may be on educational background and published papers. In publishing or public relations, a resume might have a narrative style or show a certain creative flair in the writing. A law firm or a public accounting firm might expect a very formal or conservative resume.

If you are about to graduate from college and do not have a substantial work history, you may want to emphasize your education. Include *special* classes that you feel have a bearing on your marketability, any awards or honors you received, and any special responsibilities and involvements in organizations. Provide more than just a listing of names or titles. Think in terms of skills and knowledge gained to illustrate how and why this item of experience is important to the position you are trying to obtain. If you supported yourself while in school, mention this. The best format for students is the functional resume—it allows you to present your accomplishments without emphasizing the types of jobs you held. Examples of two formats that may be useful for student resumes follow.

Harcourt Brace & Company

Resume Format #1

YOUR NAME
ADDRESS AND PHONE

Objective

Summary

Education

UNIVERSITY	DEGREE	DATE

Educational and Work-Related Accomplishments

-

-

-

-

Work History

JOB TITLE	DATES OF EMPLOYMENT
COMPANY	
JOB TITLE	DATES OF EMPLOYMENT
COMPANY	

Harcourt Brace & Company

Resume Format #2

YOUR NAME
ADDRESS AND PHONE

Objective

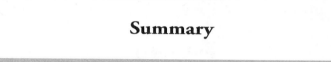

Summary

Academic Accomplishments

UNIVERSITY	DEGREE	DATE

Work History and Accomplishments

JOB TITLE	DATES OF EMPLOYMENT
COMPANY	

JOB TITLE	DATES OF EMPLOYMENT
COMPANY	

Harcourt Brace & Company

Writing the Objective

Almost every reader wants to know right away what you are looking for. Therefore, many authorities recommend that you begin with a clearly stated Job Objective that defines the kind of job you want. This objective can be very broad or very specific. Several examples of objectives follow.

A position in marketing that would utilize my technical communications experience and capitalize on my ability to communicate effectively with customers.

A position that utilizes my business training and broad experience in oil industry operations.

An internship opportunity with a dynamic, growth oriented public relations firm or department which would utilize my project development experience and enhance my ongoing MBA program.

If you are pursuing several different types of positions, *do not* include two objectives on the same resume. Instead, develop two resumes with different objectives at the top, or even completely different resumes, with different objectives and accomplishments. When possible, a relevant and company-specific objective should be utilized.

Always include an objective. Otherwise, you force the recruiter or selection specialist to "figure out" where you belong in the company. If I have 500 resumes to evaluate, I'm not going to take the time to "figure out" where you belong.

Also, do not use the term *entry level* in your objective. What if I don't have any entry level jobs? I'll immediately eliminate you from a secondary level position—even if you might be qualified. Don't overly restrict yourself. A final point on writing your objective: Do not copy it from this exercise or from a resume writing book. If you do, it will sound just like all the rest.

Writing a Summary

The summary explains in a few lines who you are and why you deserve the job mentioned in your objective. In other words, it summarizes your credentials, skills, and qualifications—as they relate to your job objective. One paragraph of four to eight lines is usually enough. If the summary gets too long, you can break it down into subsections with bullets. Several examples of summaries follow.

Five years' experience in project development, cost forecasting and economic analysis. Areas of expertise include:

- Project planning
- Program implementation
- Computer skills
- Report writing
- Oral presentation skills

Over fifteen years' production experience at various domestic locations with direct responsibility for a broad range of technical functions, including equipment installations, waterfloods, steam operations, workovers, and recompletions. Extensive field experience in conjunction with this work.

Harcourt Brace & Company

Fourteen years' experience, including nine years in the telecommunications industry and four years in a supervisory capacity. Skills include:

- Problem solving
- Communication and systems analysis
- Customer relations
- Project development

For individuals possessing little or no experience, such as a new college graduate, you might consider using a profile or highlight in place of the paragraph format. Examples of three different student profiles follow.

Professional Profile

- Well developed oral and written communication skills
- Dependable and willing to accept responsibilities
- Proven organizational and leadership skills
- Goal-oriented, confident, professional

Professional Profile

- Outstanding academic achievement (3.88/4.00)
- Well developed written and oral communication skills
- Proven organizational and problem solving skills
- Responsible, friendly, and thorough

Highlights of Qualifications

- 100% self-financed my college education
- Excelled at balancing work and academic responsibilities
- Functional with Lotus 1-2-3, Microsoft Word, and WordPerfect
- Self-motivated, responsible, and hard-working

Highlighting Academic and Work Accomplishments

You may want to use two separate categories if you have a rather impressive work history or many academic accomplishments. List several accomplishments. Try to use accomplishments that support your objective and summary. Your accomplishments should come from those identified in the preceding exercise. They should be concise and begin with an action verb.

Employment History—or Working Experience—or Career Background

For recent jobs it is usually worthwhile to list each job assignment within each company. A good framework begins with the job title followed by the approximate dates, the company name and your accomplishment(s). The amount of detail for each job should taper down as you move farther back in your career.

Harcourt Brace & Company

Work History and Accomplishments

JOB TITLE   DATES OF EMPLOYMENT
COMPANY

If you are highlighting your accomplishments and simply including a work history, group your accomplishments under a functional heading and use the framework described earlier to list your jobs.

Educational and Work-Related Accomplishments

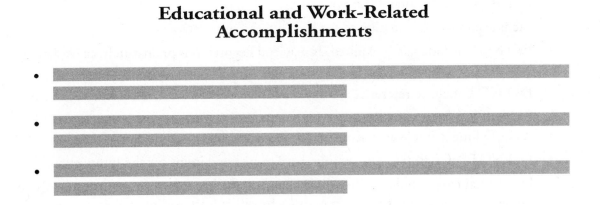

Work History

JOB TITLE   DATES OF EMPLOYMENT
COMPANY

JOB TITLE   DATES OF EMPLOYMENT
COMPANY

Summarizing Your Education

If you are just graduating and have very little work experience, education might be right near the top of your resume. But for most commercial or industrial jobs, it can come at the end. This is also a good place to list supplementary training you have received, such as workshops, conferences, seminars, special courses, etc. For example:

1995   B.S./Applied Computer Science at Illinois State University

1994   Harvard University—Thirteen-week general management course

If you are emphasizing your education (placing it at the beginning of the resume), you may want to use a slightly different format. For example:

Harcourt Brace & Company

B.B.A.   Illinois State University - May, 1996
              Area of Concentration: Human Resource Management

Illinois State University   B.B.A.–May, 1996
                                 Magna Cum Laude
                                 Major: Marketing

You may decide to include a special section related to academic awards or honors and accomplishments (as discussed earlier). You may also want to include memberships in organizations, especially if they are related to the type of work you are seeking.

A Few More Helpful Hints

- Present yourself accurately and positively.

- Include enough information to get the "buyer's" interest.

- DO NOT include salary required. It may end negotiations prematurely. Have a range in mind for face-to-face discussion after you have the lay of the land.

- DO NOT include references. That comes later when parties both agree there is strong interest.

- AVOID long, complicated sentences or paragraphs.

- DO NOT "over-stuff" your resume. Save some good items for the interview.

- Use capital letters, bullets, underlining, and so forth, to dress up your resume. Use underlining with care as it can sometimes be difficult to read on copies.

- Have several people proofread your resume before printing.

- Smaller type will permit more on a page without looking crowded, Play with fonts and margins to get the best layout. RESUMES SHOULD BE NO LONGER THAN ONE PAGE.

The following are the most common faults observed by professional resume readers:

- Failure to state a clear objective early on the resume.

- Failure to describe any accomplishments.

- Using an objective for which the applicant is obviously unqualified.

- Wordiness, incorrect spelling, and bad grammar.

- Incomplete employment history.

- Poor layout, paper, and general appearance.

THE EXERCISE ASSIGNMENT

Write an accomplishments-oriented resume for yourself. Decide on a general format. Pull together a draft and get someone to help you critique and revise it. You should expect to go through several revisions.

Harcourt Brace & Company

The final resume that you hand in for this assignment must be typed on a single sheet of paper. We suggest that you use a word processor and save the final copy on disk in order to facilitate future revisions. Remember, your resume is an evolving reflection of you. As you continue your job search it may need to be improved, or the objective may need to be changed. These types of changes are natural as your job search continues.

Harcourt Brace & Company

WRITTEN COMMUNICATION SKILLS
EXPERIENTIAL EXERCISE 8.5
Resume Writing III:
Developing a Marketing Letter

OBJECTIVE: You will write a cover letter to accompany your personal resume.

The Role of Marketing Letters in Your Job Search

Good marketing letters can supplement and work in tandem with your networking and other search techniques. In your letter approach to any company, the ultimate purpose is to get an interview. The first response to your letter may be a phone or written request for more information. Make the letter interesting enough to provoke a request for more information.

There are several different types of letters you can use in your job search process:

- The *search letter* tends to be more of a cover letter summarizing briefly your objective and background and referring to the attached resume.

- The *company broadcast letter* will give you more room for creative writing since it usually tells your story without a resume.

- The *customized* or *personalized letter* is aimed at a particular company and individual, usually someone that you have selected as a target. It is a rifle letter, not a shotgun. Often it is designed to stand on its own without an attached resume.

- The *follow-up letter* is usually just an informal note. For example, it may convey your thanks and your enjoyment of an interview. It may attempt to get closure regarding the next step. Or it may be simply a reminder that you are still interested.

Your marketing letter should always include a resume unless you are sending a follow-up letter.

Reach the Right Person

Finding the correct person to write to is an important part of your task. Companies and top executives are flooded with letters and resumes, so they each develop their own way of handling them. Most commonly, an executive who receives this flood of mail will ask his or her secretary (or some other gatekeeper) to screen it. Gatekeepers may:

- Throw your letter in the trash.
- Send it to Personnel or Human Resources.

Harcourt Brace & Company

- Buck it down the ladder or to another department or division.

- Put it in the boss's mail pile.

- Call it to the boss's attention because it looks interesting.

Your real challenge is to address your letter to a person who takes a keen interest in hiring your type of talent. If you have experience and are seeking a job in a specific function, your best bet is to address the letter to the executive in charge of that function. Otherwise, you should probably address your letter to the human resources manager (make sure you confirm the name).

In searching for marketing and sales positions, many students have been successful in identifying the proper contact person within a specific target company by first finding that company's products in the marketplace. With this as a starting point, they begin working backwards through the various intermediaries until they find the information they are seeking. The following is an example of the backwards process used successfully by one student:

> In preparing for her job search, Jamie Smith identified Flexall Industries as one of her primary target companies. Jamie did not have any networks into Flexall and the company had never recruited at her university. Nevertheless, the information that Jamie had been acquiring about the company did identify several of its products by name. Knowing these products were sold to hospitals and pharmacies, Jamie called on several hospital purchasing offices and local pharmacies. It took perseverance, but she walked out with the name and address of Jim Burnett, the salesperson responsible for that region. After several calls, she finally made contact with Jim.
>
> Naturally, he was guarded at first, but Jamie was careful to establish up front that she just wanted to talk about Flexall and was not asking for an employment interview with him. After several minutes of small talk, Jamie offered to buy Jim coffee the next time he was in town calling on his accounts. He not only accepted but also paid for the coffee. During their meeting, Jamie got a lot of information that she could never have found in the career resources library or the Flexall Annual Report. Included with this information was the name and address of the national sales director having primary responsibility for recruiting and hiring as well as the name and address of a district manager who was actively recruiting to fill a vacancy.
>
> Jamie responded by sending a marketing letter and resume to both individuals (different letters, by the way). You might be interested in a couple of points. First, Jamie is working for Flexall—and has been ranked as one of their top performing rookies! Second, about two weeks into the training program, the national sales director let her know that her ingenuity in finding a way to make contact with the company was one of the chief reasons she got the job offer. It had something to do with ". . . that's what we are looking for in our salespeople."

Once you identify who to contact, make sure the information is current and correct. The directories you read can easily be a year or two old, and companies tend to move people around. Your chances of getting through are greatly improved if your letter is correctly addressed to a responsible person, with the correct spelling and title. There is only one way to be sure of this: Call the headquarters, saying, "I would like to write a letter to _____. Is he or she still V.P. of _____? Can you help me with the exact spelling of his or her name and initials? Is he or she still located at this address?" If the telephone operator or receptionist does not sound well informed, try the Personnel Department.

Harcourt Brace & Company

Admittedly, this double-checking is all very time consuming, but it will increase your yield of inquiries or interviews.

Writing the Marketing Letter

The opening paragraph counts most. It must hook the executive's attention with something that he or she wants to hear about—something that touches on his or her needs.

- Note that this paragraph is *not* about what *you* need.
- Most often it will describe an accomplishment that relates to the sort of job you are seeking.
- Or it may be one of the other attention-getting devices described below.

Typical strategies include the corporate needs and accomplishments approach, the direct approach, the narrative approach, the current events approach, and the provocative approach. Examples of each approach follow:

The Corporate Needs and Accomplishments Approach. Here you describe a problem that is common to your industry, how you tackled it, and what results you got. This approach gets right to the meat of why people might want to hire you.

The Direct Approach. You tell briefly in the first paragraph who you are and what you seek. This may be very similar to the first half-page of your resume. This approach works well if you are just naturally marketable—you are the right age, you are a high achiever, you have a great track record, and you come from well-known companies.

The Tell a Story or Narrative Approach. Here you tell about yourself in narrative fashion, incorporating something unusual or very interesting that has happened to you recently.

The Current Events Approach. You relate your recent experience to something going on in the industry that is of wide interest.

The Provocative Approach. The first paragraph must contain something startling. Example: "I've just been fired and realize it was a good thing," or "I'd be willing to work for no salary if you would give me half of the utility costs I can save you." This approach is a bit risky unless it is carried off well.

Guidelines

In writing your marketing letter, there are several general guidelines you should incorporate. Some of these guidelines follow:

- Sell your accomplishments and your relevant experience.
- Don't go back too far.
- Omit personal data, such as age, hobbies, marital status, or children (unless they relate directly to the job).

Harcourt Brace & Company

- Omit salary, past or desired.

- Omit employment dates—in fact, all dates.

- Omit the common resume references. Use a reference in the marketing letter only if it is a person who suggested you write this letter.

- Plan on sweating through several drafts. Polish them!!!! Mistakes—spelling or grammar—will kill your chances!!

THE EXERCISE ASSIGNMENT

Develop and craft a marketing letter to accompany your resume. Use one of the approaches discussed earlier. Your final drafts must be typed as if they were to be mailed. Again, using a word processor and saving your files on disk are highly recommended.

MODULE NINE

STRATEGIC PROSPECTING SKILLS

Strategic prospecting involves the identification of qualified potential customers, usually called prospects. When we say a prospect is qualified, it means that the prospect meets or exceeds screening criteria that has been established by the salesperson or the sales organization. For example, qualified prospects must be compatible with sales strategy. A low-price buyer is inconsistent with a selling strategy that commands a premium price for a high-quality product, and thus would be eliminated as a prospect. While Kmart would be compatible with the selling strategy of many clothing companies, it would not be compatible with the selling strategies of Tommy Hilfiger or Liz Claiborne, two companies that seek a limited number of upscale retail distribution outlets rather than a low-price mass distribution system such as Kmart.

Prospects must also meet criteria such as being financially capable of making the purchase, able to truly benefit from what is being sold, accessible to the salesperson, and in a position to make or support a purchase decision. In addition to these common criteria, it is likely that salespeople or their companies will impose additional criteria for qualifying prospects.

Prospecting is extremely important to most salespeople. Salespeople who do not regularly prospect are operating under the assumption that the current customer base will be sufficient to generate the desired level of future revenue. This is a shaky assumption in that market conditions may change, causing existing customers to buy less. Another possibility is that customers may go out of business, or be bought by another firm with buying offices outside the salesperson's territory. The salesperson may simply lose customers due to competitive activity or dissatisfaction with the product, the salesperson, or the selling firm. Since there is typically a considerable time lag between the commencement of prospecting and the conversion of prospects to customer status, salespeople should spend some time prospecting on a regular basis. Otherwise, lost sales volume cannot be regained quickly enough to satisfy the large majority of sales organizations—those that are growth-oriented.

Harcourt Brace & Company

In the midst of the current knowledge and technological explosion, information about prospective customers is readily available. For example, cumbersome printed directories have been replaced by computer disks or on-line services. These computerized directories can be easily searched for specific keyword criteria, and prospects can be categorized by size, location, and many other variables. Some computerized directories can be linked with mapping software so that it is possible to identify the number of prospects in different geographic locations. This is only one example of how salespeople learn about prospects. With all the different prospecting methods available (you will learn about these in this module), it is important that salespeople have a prospecting plan or system.

A prospecting plan should fit the individual needs of the salesperson and include specific objectives for numbers of new prospects in a specified time period. The plan should also allocate an adequate amount of time on a daily or weekly basis for prospecting activities. Within the plan, allowances should be made for experimentation with different prospecting methods in order to find the most productive means of finding prospects. A tracking system should be part of the plan to assist in planning and execution of sales activities as the prospect is moved toward customer status. Periodically, the plan should be reviewed and modifications made to ensure future productivity.

As with all phases of the sales process, salespeople must exercise judgment and set priorities in prospecting. There is a limited amount of time for prospecting, and a better understanding of the concepts and practices illustrated in the module can help a salesperson be more productive. An added bonus is that the sales process is more enjoyable for salespeople who call on bona fide prospects who can benefit from the salesperson's offering.

Experiential Exercise 9.1 (*How Successful and Poor Salespeople Spend Their Time*) provides information on how important prospecting is to salespeople. In Experiential Exercise 9.2 (*Prospecting for Clients*), you will identify sources of information and develop a list of prospects for copy machines. You will also specify the type of information about the prospects that will be needed for subsequent sales calls. Five customer contact methods (in-person, form letter, telephone, personalized letters, and e-mail) are your choices for achieving sales outcomes in Experiential Exercise 9.3 (*Assessing the Effectiveness of Different Customer Contact Methods*). There are 14 outcomes, including getting an initial appointment, confirming an appointment, creating awareness of your product, company, and discovering customer needs. The final exercise in this module, Experiential Exercise 9.4 (*Prospecting Effectiveness*), gives you an understanding of some popular prospecting methods and gives you practice in matching these methods to different selling situations.

STRATEGIC PROSPECTING SKILLS
EXPERIENTIAL EXERCISE 9.1
How Successful and Poor Salespeople Spend Their Time

OBJECTIVE: You will be able to determine how important prospecting is to the successful salesperson.

INTRODUCTION

Your success in sales is more closely related to your ability to *get* information than to your ability to *give* information. The key to effective prospecting is the ability and willingness to get enough information so you can determine if you have a bona fide prospect. The most successful salespeople spend quite a bit of their time prospecting.

   Research by Tim Connor has identified six areas in which salespeople spend most of their time. These areas are identified below. Based on your understanding and experience, estimate the amount of time both poor and successful salespeople spend in each of these areas.

THE EXERCISE ASSIGNMENT

Using 100 points for each salesperson (poor and successful), divide these total points among the six areas of attention (that is, a poor salesperson spends 15% of her or his time prospecting, 15% in sales presentations, 15% in service, 15% in administration, 25% in travel, and 15% in self-improvement.)

POOR SALESPEOPLE	AREAS OF ATTENTION	SUCCESSFUL SALESPEOPLE
_____	Prospecting	_____
_____	Sales Presentation	_____
_____	Service	_____
_____	Administration	_____
_____	Travel	_____
_____	Self-improvement	_____

Harcourt Brace & Company

STRATEGIC PROSPECTING SKILLS
EXPERIENTIAL EXERCISE 9.2
Prospecting for Clients

OBJECTIVE: You will be able to establish a procedure for prospecting in a new territory.

THE EXERCISE ASSIGNMENT

You have recently graduated from college and are selling a new line with X-tra Clear Copiers. You have been assigned to a new territory in a city of 100,000 near your campus. You do not have any clients who currently own X-tra Clear Copiers. Your boss asks you to develop a prospecting list in 10 days. How might you go about generating this list of prospects?

Provide a list of sources you might use to generate leads.

1. _____
2. _____
3. _____
4. _____
5. _____
6. _____
7. _____
8. _____
9. _____
10. _____

Provide a list of establishments that would be prospects for X-tra Clear Copiers. Can you identify a person to call on? What information should you try to collect?

1. Company _____
   Who to call on _____
   Info to collect _____

MODULE NINE Strategic Prospecting Skills

2. Company _____
   Who to call on _____
   Info to collect _____

3. Company _____
   Who to call on _____
   Info to collect _____

4. Company _____
   Who to call on _____
   Info to collect _____

5. Company _____
   Who to call on _____
   Info to collect _____

6. Company _____
   Who to call on _____
   Info to collect _____

7. Company _____
   Who to call on _____
   Info to collect _____

8. Company _____
   Who to call on _____
   Info to collect _____

9. Company _____
   Who to call on _____
   Info to collect _____

10. Company _____
    Who to call on _____
    Info to collect _____

Harcourt Brace & Company

STRATEGIC PROSPECTING SKILLS
EXPERIENTIAL EXERCISE 9.3
Assessing the Effectiveness of Different Customer Contact Methods

OBJECTIVE: You will develop your understanding of the various methods for making customer contact and how each method's effectiveness varies according to desired outcomes.

THE EXERCISE ASSIGNMENT

The effectiveness of the various methods available for salespeople to make contact with prospects and customers will vary according to what the salesperson hopes to accomplish. This exercise requires that you consider certain outcomes that a salesperson might desire and designate which contact method(s) might be the most effective. To encourage your thoughtful consideration of each method's strengths and weaknesses, the exercise also requires you to explain why you made your selections.

EVALUATING THE EFFECTIVENESS OF CUSTOMER CONTACT METHODS

For each of the following desired outcomes, indicate which customer contact method would be the best to use. Indicate your choice by entering the letter(s) corresponding to the chosen contact method(s):

In Person (P)   E-mail (E)
Form Letter (F)   Personalized Letter (L)
Telephone (T)   World-Wide Web (W)

After you have made your selection, briefly explain why you believe this to be the optimal choice. This information will be used for class discussion.

METHOD

Creating awareness of product or company.   _____

Why: _____

_____

_____

Harcourt Brace & Company

METHOD

Introducing yourself.   _____

Why? _____

_____

_____

Providing detailed product information.   _____

Why? _____

_____

_____

Summarizing a specific proposal.   _____

Why? _____

_____

_____

Closing a sale.   _____

Why? _____

_____

_____

Getting an initial appointment.   _____

Why? _____

_____

_____

Getting a follow-up appointment.   _____

Why? _____

_____

_____

Confirming an appointment.   _____

Why? _____

_____

_____

Harcourt Brace & Company

METHOD

Getting acquainted.   _____

Why? _____

_____

_____

Building your credibility.   _____

Why? _____

_____

_____

Demonstrating products.   _____

Why? _____

_____

_____

Discovering customer needs.   _____

Why? _____

_____

_____

Confirming a major point.   _____

Why? _____

_____

_____

Confirming a minor point.   _____

Why? _____

_____

_____

Harcourt Brace & Company

STRATEGIC PROSPECTING SKILLS
EXPERIENTIAL EXERCISE 9.4
Prospecting Effectiveness

OBJECTIVE: You will be able to identify prospecting techniques and determine the effectiveness of the techniques.

THE EXERCISE ASSIGNMENT

Some of the best ways to identify potential prospects are through the use of external sources, internal sources, personal contacts, and others. Your class materials, lecture, and discussion will provide you with a number of different techniques for each of these broad categories. Based on your understanding of the different prospecting techniques, identify and discuss how you would use these different techniques in relation to the identified sources.

CATEGORY OF SOURCES   PROSPECTING TECHNIQUE

1. External Sources
    _____

    _____

    _____

    _____

    _____

    _____

2. Internal Sources
    _____

    _____

    _____

3. Personal Contact
    _____

    _____

4. Miscellaneous
    _____

    _____

    _____

Harcourt Brace & Company

List each prospecting method described above and record your opinion of its effectiveness.

1. Prospecting method _____

    In your opinion, what is the strength or weakness of this prospecting method?

    _____

    _____

    _____

2. Prospecting method _____

    In your opinion, what is the strength or weakness of this prospecting method?

    _____

    _____

3. Prospecting method _____

    In your opinion, what is the strength or weakness of this prospecting method?

    _____

    _____

    _____

4. Prospecting method _____

    In your opinion, what is the strength or weakness of this prospecting method?

    _____

    _____

    _____

Adapted from Ingram, T. N. SMEI *Certification Study Guide,* The University of Memphis: SMEI Accreditation Institute, 1994.

MODULE TEN

SALES PRESENTATION SKILLS

Reflecting the emphasis of today's adaptive selling and relationship marketing philosophies, a great deal of this text (that is, Modules 5, 6, and 7) has focused on communication, questioning, and listening skills. Earlier approaches like AIDA and Stimulus-Response put the buyer through a structured series of steps that generally dealt with one-way communication. The emphasis in selling today is on Adaptive Selling and Relationship Selling. Today's focus is on a more balanced approach in which the buyer and seller are viewed as equals working together to create opportunities and solve problems. Effective communication techniques are critical to today's salesperson as they must ask questions, interview the buyer, listen, and respond to the *specific* needs of each buyer. Thus, the salesperson must select only those features and benefits of the product that are relevant to the identified needs of the buyer.

For decades, salespeople have been exhorted to "sell the sizzle, not the steak," and to remember that "when the customer says no, you are just beginning to sell." Such advice rings hollow as we move into the next decade of professional selling. Although dramatic and emotionally charged sales presentations may be quite effective on certain occasions (for example, trade shows), they are not likely to consistently produce sales unless the rational motives of the prospect have been given primary consideration.

In contrast to the stereotypical bare-knuckle, song-and-dance, personality-plus sales relics of the past, the contemporary professional salesperson relies more on printed sales support material, audio-visual aids, and sales technologies, such as laptop computers. Research indicates that the visual and vocal elements of a sales message are more memorable than the actual content of the message. Consequently, effective salespeople use every clarity enhancing tool at their disposal. By being knowledgeable about their products, the competition, and their customers' needs, successful salespeople are able to adapt readily to the situation—without appearing to be self-serving, transparent chameleons who mirror every movement of the prospect.

The exercises in this module are designed to enhance your understanding of appropriate sales presentation skills. Experiential Exercise 10.1 (*Developing Feature and Benefit*

Harcourt Brace & Company

Statements for Your University) will help you develop specific benefit statements for specific markets at your university. Any feature may produce different benefits for different student markets and no benefits for others. The more precisely you can express the benefit in the language of the student market, the more effective your statements will be.

Experiential Exercises 10.2 (*Presentation Effectiveness—Discussion Questions*) and 10.4 (*Helpful Hints for Sales Presentations*) ask you questions pertaining to sales presentation tactics, such as: How long should a good presentation be? Why should I get the customer involved? Should I ever argue with the customer even if I am right? After you answer and discuss these questions, you will have a better understanding of the do's and don'ts of successful presentations.

All salespeople must do some planning before they present to their customer or prospect. You will be asked to develop an in-depth plan in Experiential Exercise 10.3 (*Sales Call Planning Report*). Here you will develop feature/benefit statements; identify your company and product; profile the competition and the prospect; anticipate problems and objections; and determine methods for gaining commitment and follow-up. This thorough plan may be used as the setup for your final class presentation.

In addition to the actual presentation, your appearance and manner when you meet a prospect for the first time must convey a favorable impression. Within the first few minutes you and the prospect are together, the prospect makes judgments that will have a direct effect on the interaction to follow. Communication research suggests that both educational and persuasive communications are more effective under conditions in which the buyer has greater involvement in the presentation rather than being a passive observer. However, creating opportunities for buyer involvement often takes some thought and encouragement on the part of the salesperson. Experiential Exercises 10.5 (*Initiating the Sales Conversation by Getting the Customer's Attention*) and 10.6 (*Generating Buyer Involvement*) provide help in getting the sales conversation started and the buyer involved.

SALES PRESENTATION SKILLS
EXPERIENTIAL EXERCISE 10.1
*Developing Feature and Benefit Statements
for Your School*

INTRODUCTION

Benefit statements describe a feature from a specific customer's point of view. They answer such customer questions as "How is this going to help *me* solve *my* problems?"

Any given feature may produce different benefits for different customers and no benefits for others. Therefore, it's important to develop benefit statements for specific markets. The more precisely you can express the benefit *in the language of the customer,* the more effective your statements will be. The following example will help you get started on this assignment.

Example

The following example will help you understand this exercise. First, choose three groups that represent target markets at your school (examples could be: Greeks, athletes, handicap students, faculty, staff, graduate students, general student population, freshmen, and so on).

1. Target Market (*for example, athletes*)
2. Target Market (*for example, handicap students*)
3. Target Market (*for example, graduate students*)

Next, select a feature of your school (an example might be a tutoring program available at your school).

1. Feature: *Tutoring program available to our students.*

Finally, develop a benefit statement for each of your target markets. Remember, any given feature may produce different benefits for one target group and no benefit for the others.

Target Market 1. *athletes*   Benefit Statement: *Athletes spend time at practice and away games, the benefit of the tutoring program to the athlete is they can use the program to catch up on their work and not fall behind.*

OBJECTIVE: You will be able to develop feature and benefit statements for your school and apply them to relevant markets.

Harcourt Brace & Company

Market 2. *handicap students*   Benefit Statement: *Students who are blind have readers available to read lessons to them. The benefit to the students is they do not have to pay for a reader.*

Market 3. *graduate students*   Benefit Statement: *Graduate students are used as the tutors. The benefit to the grad student is they can supplement their income and feel good about helping others.*

THE EXERCISE ASSIGNMENT

Based on the example provided, develop additional features and benefit statements for your three target markets.

1. Feature: _____

    Target Market 1: _____   Benefit Statement: _____

_____

_____

    Target Market 2: _____   Benefit Statement: _____

_____

    Target Market 3: _____   Benefit Statement: _____

_____

_____

2. Feature: _____

    Target Market 1: _____   Benefit Statement: _____

_____

_____

    Target Market 2: _____   Benefit Statement: _____

_____

_____

    Target Market 3: _____   Benefit Statement: _____

_____

_____

Harcourt Brace & Company

3. Feature: _____

    Target Market 1: _____   Benefit Statement: _____

_____

_____

    Target Market 2: _____   Benefit Statement: _____

_____

_____

    Target Market 3: _____   Benefit Statement: _____

_____

_____

4. Feature: _____

    Target Market 1: _____   Benefit Statement: _____

_____

_____

    Target Market 2: _____   Benefit Statement: _____

_____

_____

    Target Market 3: _____   Benefit Statement: _____

_____

_____

5. Feature: _____

    Target Market 1: _____   Benefit Statement: _____

_____

_____

    Target Market 2: _____   Benefit Statement: _____

_____

_____

    Target Market 3: _____   Benefit Statement: _____

_____

_____

Harcourt Brace & Company

6. Feature: _____

    Target Market 1: _____ Benefit Statement: _____

    _____

    Target Market 2: _____ Benefit Statement: _____

    _____

    Target Market 3: _____ Benefit Statement: _____

    _____

7. Feature: _____

    Target Market 1: _____ Benefit Statement: _____

    _____

    Target Market 2: _____ Benefit Statement: _____

    _____

    Target Market 3: _____ Benefit Statement: _____

    _____

8. Feature: _____

    Target Market 1: _____ Benefit Statement: _____

    _____

    Target Market 2: _____ Benefit Statement: _____

    _____

    Target Market 3: _____ Benefit Statement: _____

    _____

Harcourt Brace & Company

SALES PRESENTATION SKILLS
EXPERIENTIAL EXERCISE 10.2
Presentation Effectiveness— Discussion Questions

OBJECTIVE: You will be able to think through the presentation and to understand its key components.

THE EXERCISE ASSIGNMENT

Please respond to the following statements:

1. What is the main objective of a good presentation? _____
    _____
    _____

2. How long should a good presentation be? _____
    _____
    _____

3. Why are questions an important part of a presentation? _____
    _____
    _____
    _____

4. When should you terminate a presentation? _____
    _____
    _____

5. How should you terminate a sales call? _____
    _____
    _____

Harcourt Brace & Company

SALES PRESENTATION SKILLS
EXPERIENTIAL EXERCISE 10.3
Sales Call Planning Report

OBJECTIVE: You will build your understanding of the importance of thorough strategic planning prior to calling on the customer by illustrating the integra-
tion of sales call objectives, features and benefits (FAB), and the ADAPT
questioning process.

INTRODUCTION

Successful selling is based on thorough planning and preparation *before* the sales call and
presentation. One of the most important areas of preparation pertains to understanding a
product's features and how they might solve buyer needs. The link between product features and buyer needs is accomplished by converting a product's *FEATURES (what it is)*
to *ADVANTAGES (what it does),* and then translating these advantages into *BENEFITS
that are relevant and meaningful to your buyer.*

Benefits are solutions to needs. It is important to realize that specific features may yield
different benefits to different buyers. Thus, preparation includes imagining the variety of
buyer needs that a feature might address and how to uncover potential benefits through
questioning. Such preparation forces the salesperson to cognitively examine prospects in
terms of:

1. product features that might give rise to buyer benefits

2. ADAPT questions to use in assessing the prospect's needs in relation to available
   product benefits

3. potential resistance in accepting and committing to the benefits as solutions to the
   prospect's problems and needs.

THE EXERCISE ASSIGNMENT

Unlike the other experiential exercises in this workbook in which the scenario was already
set out for you, this exercise requires that you develop your own selling scenario, including (a) the product being sold, (b) the company you sell for, and (c) the prospect to whom
you are selling. These product, company, and prospect profiles will then be used to anticipate the events and responses within a sales call in order to develop a detailed, strategic plan
for making that call. All this will come together in a formal written report consisting of certain specific components.

Harcourt Brace & Company

We recommend that this assignment be done in groups of two students. You may exchange ideas, work through the various parts of the report together, and turn in one report. The assignment will be evaluated in terms of its preparation as well as its content. The report must be typed, professional in appearance and double spaced with one-inch margins. Headings, subheadings, and page numbers should be used to organize the report. A comb binder (for example, Kinko's or PIP's) should be used rather than a plastic slip-on cover. The front cover should creatively, professionally, and neatly identify the specific product the report addresses, the members of the sales team, and the project due date. Inside, the report should consist of the following major sections:

Letter of Transmittal Assuming that your sales manager has requested a copy of your sales call plan, the first component of your report should be a letter of transmittal addressed to your sales manager (your instructor). Similar to an executive summary, this letter of transmittal references the manager's request, identifies your subject prospect along with the time and place of the sales call appointment, establishes the specific objectives you have set for this sales call, and provides a synopsis of the report's contents. This letter should be single-spaced and limited to one page.

Identification of Your Company This section profiles the company for which you sell. Actual companies may be used if you desire. This portion of the report develops detailed information, such as the name of the company, its size, and a brief history. Other information should also be included that might be relevant to a buyer. This information will facilitate the profile's use should it be used in a subsequent buyer–seller role play.

Identification of Your Product Choose a good or service that you would like to sell. (You might consider using a product from a company that you might want to go to work for, as this project can be quite beneficial to you in your job interviews.) All products are to be sold to another business or institution. Sales of products to individuals for their own use is not allowed. Experience indicates that the closer a product is to the retail marketplace, the harder it is to use, and the closer the product is to being industrial in nature, the better it seems to work. Your product choice should be in good taste and legal, and must not be in conflict with any school rules or policies.

The last portion of this section should be a chart of the product's general features, advantages, and benefits. To assist you in developing this information, an example of an FAB chart is included at the end of this exercise.

Profile of Competition Who are the major competitors? What are their strengths and weaknesses? How do competitive products compare to the FABs of your product? This section must develop and describe at least two competitors.

Profile of Prospect This section profiles both the buyer and the buyer's company. What is the name of the person you are calling on? What is his or her position and history with the firm? What is the company name and type of business? Where are they located? What information do we know before actually making a sales call? How is our product relevant to them? Is the use for resale or manufacture? What brands and suppliers are currently being used?

Harcourt Brace & Company

Expected Problems and Needs What types of customer problems might be discovered in working with this prospect? What advance information or intelligence do you have regarding problems or needs? In this section you should develop four potential problems relevant to both your prospect and your type of product. In the following section you will use these four potential problems as a guide to develop a series of ADAPT questions that would address these problems and ascertain corresponding needs.

Develop ADAPT Question Sequence As a major part of this section, you should develop and include a series of product and customer relevant questions that can be used to assess the needs of your prospects. These questions should follow the ADAPT questioning sequence (explained in Module 6, Questioning Skills). Workbook pages for developing ADAPT questions are included on pages 195–196. Keep in mind that the ADAPT sequence of questions is intended to help your prospect discover and solve a problem, as opposed to "pitching" a product.

Expected Objections and Resistance What forms of resistance are expected? This section should detail ten specific objections that you expect in making your presentation to this account. Classify each of these objections by type. For each objection, describe how you would respond. Classify each response by type.

Gaining Customer Commitment Describe and illustrate how you will gain customer commitment and finalize the sale. Your description should include a statement classifying the type of commitment-gaining method being used.

Customer Follow-Up This section discusses the follow-up activities that will be undertaken and provides a timetable for their implementation. Follow-up activities should be developed for both contingencies: (a) that you are successful in achieving the objectives set out for this sales call, and (b) that you are not successful in achieving the sales call objectives.

Harcourt Brace & Company

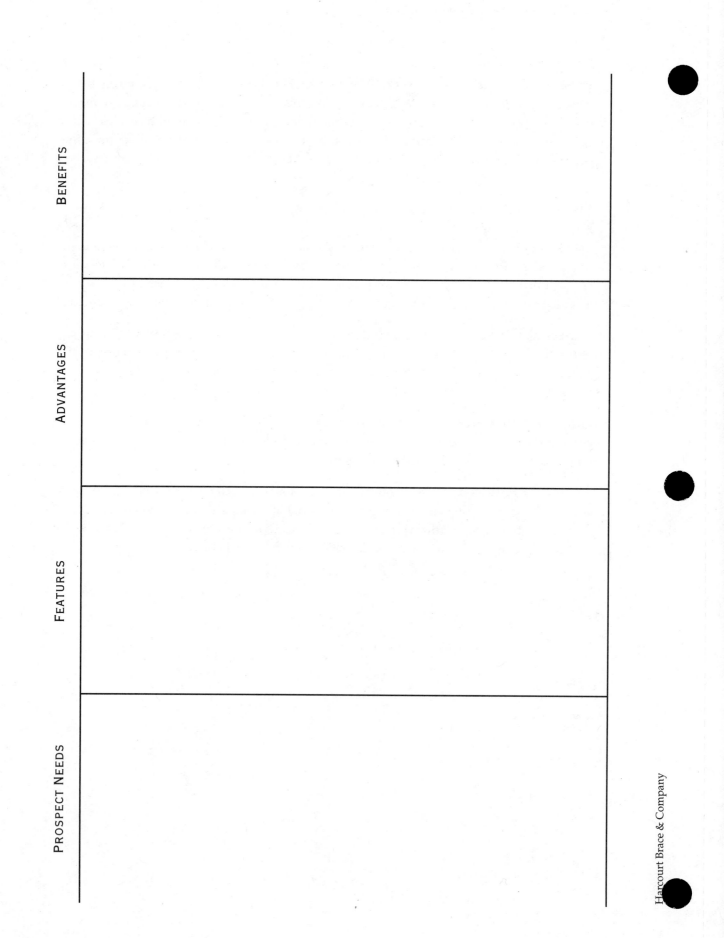

PROSPECT NEEDS | FEATURES | ADVANTAGES | BENEFITS

Harcourt Brace & Company

194

SALESPERSON'S PREPARATION FORM

Assessment Questions:

_____
_____
_____
_____
_____
_____
_____
_____
_____

Discovery Questions:

_____
_____
_____
_____
_____
_____
_____
_____
_____

Activation Questions:

_____
_____
_____
_____
_____
_____
_____
_____
_____

Harcourt Brace & Company

Projection Questions:

_____
_____
_____
_____
_____
_____
_____
_____
_____

Transition Questions:

_____
_____
_____
_____
_____
_____
_____
_____
_____

Harcourt Brace & Company

◉

SALES PRESENTATION SKILLS
EXPERIENTIAL EXERCISE 10.4
Helpful Hints for Sales Presentations

✳

OBJECTIVE: You will be able to understand some key issues that can make the sales presentation more effective.

THE EXERCISE ASSIGNMENT

Please respond to the following statements:

1. Use short, simple, uncomplicated words. Why? _____

    _____

    _____

2. Use words that create a visual image. Why? _____

    _____

    _____

3. Get the customers involved. Why? _____

    _____

    _____

4. Never argue with your customers. Why? _____

    _____

    _____

5. Work from appointments—this is the mark of a pro. Why? _____

    _____

    _____

6. Plan each presentation. Have a specific objective. Why? _____

_____

_____

_____

7. Terminate the presentation as soon as you discover the prospect does not qualify. Why?

_____

_____

_____

8. Use *questions* to control the presentation. Why? _____

_____

_____

_____

9. Increase your effectiveness—practice, practice, practice! Why? _____

_____

_____

_____

Harcourt Brace & Company

SALES PRESENTATION SKILLS
EXPERIENTIAL EXERCISE 10.5
Initiating the Sales Conversation by Getting the Customer's Attention

OBJECTIVE: You will be able to understand the importance of the first few minutes of a sales conversation.

THE EXERCISE ASSIGNMENT

The sales rep's appearance and manner must convey a favorable impression. Within the first few minutes that the prospect and the sales rep are together, the prospect makes judgments that will have a direct effect on the interaction to follow. The first few words the salesperson says set the tone of the entire presentation. There are several approaches that can be used to gain the prospect's interest and attention.

A. Introduction—The sales rep states his/her name and the name of the company.

What are the strengths and weaknesses of this opening? _____

_____

_____

B. Referral—Start out by mentioning that so-and-so suggested the prospect would be interested in your product.

What are the strengths and weaknesses of this opening? _____

_____

_____

C. Question—Asking a meaningful question gets the prospect's attention, encourages a response, and initiates two-way communication.

What are the strengths and weaknesses of this opening? _____

_____

_____

D. Benefit—Focus the prospect's attention on a product benefit.

What are the strengths and weaknesses of this opening? _____

_____

_____

E. Curiosity—Arouse interest by making an unexpected comment to intrigue the prospect.

What are the strengths and weaknesses of this opening? _____

_____

_____

F. Compliment—Offer a sincere and specific compliment.

What are the strengths and weaknesses of this opening? _____

_____

_____

G. Shock—Get attention by using a gimmick or a shocking statement.

What are the strengths and weaknesses of this opening? _____

_____

_____

H. Develop an approach that utilizes a combination of the above methods.

What are the strengths and weaknesses of this opening? _____

_____

_____

Which methods did you select to combine? _____

_____

Why? _____

_____

What are the strengths and weaknesses of this opening? _____

_____

_____

Harcourt Brace & Company

SALES PRESENTATION SKILLS
EXPERIENTIAL EXERCISE 10.6
Generating Buyer Involvement

OBJECTIVE: You will increase your skill in generating the active involvement of the prospect in the presentation.

INTRODUCTION

Communication research suggests that both educational and persuasive communications are more effective when the buyer is actively involved in the presentation rather than being a passive observer. However, creating opportunities for buyer involvement often takes some thought and encouragement on the part of the salesperson.

THE EXERCISE ASSIGNMENT

Working in groups of three, consider yourselves in each of the four following selling situations. Brainstorm different techniques you could use to involve the customer for each selling situation. Using the space provided, identify five techniques you feel would be the most effective along with a brief discussion explaining why.

SITUATION 1:   A retail salesperson for Mike's Bike Shop selling a new style, ultra-light racing bike to a racing fanatic.

Technique 1 _____

_____

Why? _____

_____

Technique 2 _____

_____

Why? _____

_____

Technique 3 _____

_____

Why? _____

_____

Technique 4 _____

_____

Why? _____

_____

Technique 5 _____

_____

Why? _____

_____

SITUATION 2: A manufacturer's representative selling a new line of ultra-light racing bicycles to the buyer for Mike's Bike Shop.

Technique 1 _____

_____

Why? _____

_____

Technique 2 _____

_____

Why? _____

_____

Technique 3 _____

_____

Why? _____

_____

Harcourt Brace & Company

Technique 4 _____

_____

Why? _____

_____

Technique 5 _____

_____

Why? _____

_____

SITUATION 3: An industrial chemical salesperson selling corrosion and acid-
proof polymer coatings to a manufacturer of acid dispensing
equipment that is used in medical research labs.

Technique 1 _____

_____

Why? _____

_____

Technique 2 _____

_____

Why? _____

_____

Technique 3 _____

_____

Why? _____

_____

Technique 4 _____

_____

Why? _____

_____

Harcourt Brace & Company

Technique 5 _____

_____

Why? _____

_____

SITUATION 4: A salesperson for General Electric Jet Engine Division presenting a high-thrust, low-noise, fuel-efficient jet engine to the buying team at American Airlines to retrofit 150 of their 727-model aircraft.

Technique 1 _____

_____

Why? _____

_____

Technique 2 _____

_____

Why? _____

_____

Technique 3 _____

_____

Why? _____

_____

Technique 4 _____

_____

Why? _____

_____

Technique 5 _____

_____

Why? _____

_____

MODULE ELEVEN

SKILLS FOR EARNING COMMITMENT AND NEGOTIATING RESISTANCE

Ultimately, a large part of most salespeople's performance evaluation is based on their ability to gain customer commitment or close sales. Because of this close relationship between compensation and getting orders, traditional selling has tended to overemphasize the importance of gaining commitment. In fact, there are those who feel just about any salesperson can find a new prospect, open a sale, or take an order. These same people infer it takes a trained, motivated and skilled professional to close a sale. They go on to say the close is the keystone to a salesperson's success and a good salesperson ought to try a new close every week so that at the end of a year the salesperson will have mastered many new ways to close the sale. This outmoded emphasis on closing skills is typical of transaction selling techniques that stress making the sale at all cost.

Another popular, but outmoded suggestion to salespeople is to "close early and often." This is particularly bad advice if the prospect is not prepared to make a decision, responds negatively to a premature attempt to consummate the sale, and then (following the principles of cognitive consistency) proceeds to reinforce the prior negative position as the salesperson plugs away, firing one closing salvo after another at the beleaguered prospect. Research tells us that it will take several sales calls to make an initial sale, so it is somewhat bewildering to still encounter such tired old battle cries as "the ABC's of selling stand for Always Be Closing."

Manipulative closing gimmicks are less likely to be effective as professional buyers grow weary with the cat-and-mouse approach to selling that is still practiced by a surprising number of salespeople. It is also surprising to find many salespeople who view their customers as combatants over whom victory is sought. Once the sale is made by salespeople who have adversarial, me-against-you attitudes, the customer is likely to be neglected as the salesperson rides off into the sunset in search of yet another battle with yet another lowly customer.

One time-honored thought that does retain contemporary relevance is that "nobody likes to be sold, but everybody likes to buy." In other words, salespeople should facilitate

Harcourt Brace & Company

decision making by pointing out a suggested course of action, but should allow the prospect plenty of mental space within which a rational decision can be reached. Taken to its logical conclusion, this means that it may be acceptable to make a sales call without asking for the order. Salespeople must be cognizant, however, of their responsibility to advance the relationship toward a profitable sale, lest they become the most dreaded of all types of salespeople—the paid conversationalist.

We have already mentioned that the salesperson has taken on the expanded roles of business consultant and relationship manager, which is not consistent with pressuring the customers until they give in and say yes. Fortunately, things have changed to the point that today's professional salesperson attempts to gain commitment when the buyer is ready to buy. The salesperson should evaluate each presentation and attempt to determine the causes of its success or failure with the customer. Experiential Exercise 11.1 (*Why People Fail to Gain Commitment*) addresses the issue of failing to gain commitment. Interestingly, research shows the number one reason why sales are not completed is the sales representative makes no attempt to gain commitment.

Certain events take place during a presentation that point toward an appropriate time to ask for commitment. Other events take place that warrant the salesperson to come back another day to conclude the sale. Experiential Exercises 11.2 (*Gaining Commitment Signals*) and 11.3 (*Gaining Commitment Caution Signals*) are designed to assist you in exploring the many gaining commitment signals that may present themselves during a presentation.

You will have an opportunity to review two sales scenarios in Experiential Exercises 11.4 (*Gaining Commitment I*) and 11.5 (*Gaining Commitment II*). In Exercise 11.4, Tammy Porter is about ready to respond to Tim Short who, after shaking hands with Tammy, states, "Let's talk boats!" Tammy now has to determine how she is going to organize her presentation, ask questions, look for buying signals, handle resistance and ask for commitment if appropriate. In Exercise 11.5, you will work in groups to develop a number of gaining commitment techniques that might be used during a sales presentation.

Experiential Exercise 11.6 (*Gaining Commitment—Discussion Questions*) presents some questions that must be thought through before the presentation. If you have answers for these questions before they occur, you will be ready to respond confidently.

NEGOTIATING RESISTANCE

Very closely related to gaining commitment is negotiating problems in sales resistance. You can look at sales resistance in one of two ways. You can view resistance as a negative and essentially give up each time you get a tough question, or you can view resistance as a positive and assume the customer is just asking for more information. If you can get the customer the right information, you can possibly resolve the objection and move closer to getting the sale. One sales manager told his salesforce, "You want the customers asking tough questions concerning price, delivery, service, and so on, because if they aren't, they probably aren't interested."

Even the best planned sales presentations will invite buyer questions and objections. Buyers have legitimate concerns to be addressed: some are seeking information or

Harcourt Brace & Company

clarification, and some seek to negotiate a better deal. Knowing that buyers will raise objections and ask tough questions suggests that successful salespeople should attempt to anticipate those areas of concern and formulate responses in advance of the sales call. In doing this, it is best to leave the bag of tricks at home and rely instead on solid, justifiable evidence. Certainly, the salesperson should learn more about listening and questioning skills, as opposed to relying on the spoken word to overcome all objections and questions. Sales trainers are finally recognizing the importance of listening, which was identified as the top sales training need in a recent survey.

The reality of competition is strongly felt in this stage of the sales process, and salespeople must be careful not to send negative signals through their responses to competitive sales practices. Buyers find it distasteful when a salesperson unduly knocks the competition. A knock on the competition is at least a partial knock on the customer.

Professional salespeople view questions and objections as opportunity, rather than as an obstacle to the sale. They are well aware that today's buyers are unlikely to prolong a sales presentation if they are not interested in buying the product or service being presented.

You will have to deal with sales resistance in almost every sales call you make. Experiential Exercise 11.7 (*Reasons for Sales Resistance*) looks at both psychological and logical sales resistance. Psychological resistance refers to an unwillingness to buy based on attitude, emotion, or prejudice. This resistance is buyer subjective and varies from one prospect to another. Logical resistance or objection to the sales presentation refers to unwillingness to buy, based on tangible considerations related to some aspect of the product. By completing this exercise you will better understand psychological and logical sales resistance and how to deal with each.

You will want to build your confidence on how to handle sales resistance. Experiential Exercise 11.8 (*LAARC: A Process for Negotiating Buyer Resistance*) is an effective process for dealing with sales resistance that was developed in industry training programs. LAARC is an acronym describing a process for you to follow in working with sales resistance.

Experiential Exercise 11.9 (*Negotiating Buyer Resistance*) will help you recognize and deal with a number of buyer resistance situations. You can apply the LAARC techniques to diagnose the area of resistance and respond to it.

Each of the Experiential Exercises in Module 11 is designed to help you think through and better understand gaining commitment and sales resistance. Better understanding of gaining commitment and resistance will help you deal with each of your prospects and customers. It is critical that you are well prepared to handle gaining commitment and sales resistance before you have to negotiate with a tough customer.

Harcourt Brace & Company

SKILLS FOR EARNING COMMITMENT
AND NEGOTIATING RESISTANCE
EXPERIENTIAL EXERCISE 11.1
Why Salespeople Fail to Gain Commitment

OBJECTIVE: You will be able to understand the issue of failure in gaining commitment.

THE EXERCISE ASSIGNMENT

One reason why sales are not completed is the sales rep makes no attempt to close the sale. Why, after investing all the time and effort in prospecting, qualifying, and making the presentation, would a sales rep not attempt to gain commitment? What are some other reasons why salespeople fail to gain commitment? Record your responses on the following lines.

1. _____

_____

2. _____

_____

3. _____

_____

4. _____

_____

5. _____

_____

6. _____

_____

Harcourt Brace & Company

SKILLS FOR EARNING COMMITMENT AND NEGOTIATING RESISTANCE
EXPERIENTIAL EXERCISE 11.2
Gaining Commitment Signals

OBJECTIVE: You will be able to recognize buying signals.

THE EXERCISE ASSIGNMENT

Please respond to the following statements:

1. The prospect makes a positive statement. Why would this be a buying signal?

    _____

    _____

    _____

2. A worried look is replaced by a happy look. Why would this be a buying signal?

    _____

    _____

    _____

3. The prospect starts playing with a pen or the order form. Why would this be a buying signal?

    _____

    _____

    _____

4. The prospect looks at the product with a favorable expression. Why would this be a buying signal?

    _____

    _____

    _____

Harcourt Brace & Company

5.　The prospect touches the product. Why would this be a buying signal?

_____

_____

_____

6.　The prospect is using or trying out the product. Why would this be a buying signal?

_____

_____

_____

7.　The prospect's tone of voice changes or his or her body relaxes. Why would this be a buying signal?

_____

_____

_____

8.　The prospect questions price, usage, or delivery. Why would this be a buying signal?

_____

_____

_____

Harcourt Brace & Company

SKILLS FOR EARNING COMMITMENT AND NEGOTIATING RESISTANCE
EXPERIENTIAL EXERCISE 11.3
Gaining Commitment Caution Signals

OBJECTIVE: You will be able to recognize gaining commitment caution signals.

INTRODUCTION

There are situations that do not warrant the salesperson attempting to gain customer commitment. It is risky to ask for the order when you are getting negative signals or when there is an indication that the prospect is uncomfortable about something. Trying to gain commitment following a negative indication without resolving the problem is being unresponsive to the prospect's need. Here are some situations where the sales rep should do something else before attempting to gain commitment.

THE EXERCISE ASSIGNMENT

Here are some situations where the sales rep should do something else before attempting to gain commitment. Examine each of the situations and explain why they should be viewed as a caution signal.

1. The prospect requests additional information on a technical product. Why would this be a buying caution signal?

    _____

    _____

    _____

2. A rushed or inadequate presentation has been made. Why would this be a buying caution signal?

    _____

    _____

    _____

Harcourt Brace & Company

3. The prospect is hostile or defensive and is not making an attempt to bargain. Why would this be a buying caution signal?

_____

_____

_____

4. The prospect raises an objection or asks for more information. Why would this be a buying caution signal?

_____

_____

_____

5. A significant interruption has disturbed the buying mood. Why would this be a buying caution signal?

_____

_____

_____

6. Gaining commitment on a minor point failed to reveal positive signs of interest. Why would this be a buying caution signal?

_____

_____

_____

SKILLS FOR EARNING COMMITMENT
AND NEGOTIATING RESISTANCE
EXPERIENTIAL EXERCISE 11.4
Gaining Commitment I

OBJECTIVE: You will develop your skills in recognizing and responding to buying signals.

THE EXERCISE ASSIGNMENT

Read the following selling situation. Visualize what has just occurred and put yourself into the role of Tammy Porter, a salesperson at Yacht Sales of America, an exclusive boat broker located on the bay just outside Houston. As you renew your acquaintance with one of your established clients, think about and respond to the four questions that follow the scenario.

Winter is almost over. In fact, down here in south Texas folks are getting an early start on spring. The weather has been in the middle to high 70s for over a month, and the mixture of sounds coming from the slip and dock areas are a sure sign that boat buying fever will soon arrive. Sure enough, traffic around the showroom has been pretty steady now for a little over a week. You are busy entering some new product information into your computer in order to send out some prospect letters, when you hear your name. It's coming from a familiar voice over by the door—and as you look around you see Tim Short, one of your best customers. In fact, Tim is interested in doing some trading and has been in several times over the past two months. The combination of all the boat activity out in the bay the last few days plus his coming in again today gives you the feeling that he is getting close to making a decision. Based on your recent conversations with Tim, you know that he:

- likes the very best that he can possibly buy.

- has excellent financing instantly available through the bank his family owns.

- wants something impressive and unique. His best friend has just traded for a new 40-foot schooner.

- is impatient and wants something for the impending season.

- plans to trade in his current boat, a 3-year-old, 38-foot schooner, for a newer, larger model.

Tim really liked the deal you made him last week on the 45-foot racing schooner. In fact, at one point you thought he was ready to buy. Nevertheless, when you tried to gain a commitment, he responded that he just wasn't sure that was the boat he wanted. He said he would think it over, and left.

Now several days later you are shaking hands with him, Tim looks you in the eye and says, "Let's talk boats!"

Harcourt Brace & Company

1. How might you organize your presentation? What will be important for you to consider?

   _____

   _____

   _____

2. What type of questioning would you start with?

   _____

   _____

   _____

   Why? _____

3. What sort of buying signals might you look for?

   _____

   _____

   _____

   Why? _____

4. What sort of resistance would you expect to encounter during the presentation?

   _____

   _____

   _____

   Why? _____

5. What techniques for gaining commitment might be appropriate?

   _____

   _____

   _____

   Why? _____

Harcourt Brace & Company

SKILLS FOR EARNING COMMITMENT AND NEGOTIATING RESISTANCE
EXPERIENTIAL EXERCISE 11.5
Gaining Commitment II

OBJECTIVE: You will develop skills in gaining customer commitment.

INTRODUCTION

You will work in groups of three and brainstorm different methods for gaining the buyer's commitment in the following selling scenario. After reading the scenario, work in your groups to develop closes that could be applied. Use the worksheets to develop and illustrate each technique listed. Notice that the worksheets also call for you to explain why you feel this is a good technique. The examples each group develops will form the basis for a class discussion.

National Payroll Corporation (NPC) is the leading provider of electronic payroll processing. Their services include a full menu of payroll services, including accounting and record keeping, check writing, and the calculation and filing of all city, state, and federal payroll taxes. Their benefits offered to clients include not only lower costs than companies incur doing it all in-house, but also higher levels of accuracy and on-time filings of the ever-increasing number of tax forms.

As a salesperson for National Payroll Corporation, you have been calling on Acme Mechanical for about seven months now. Tony Fiona, the chief financial officer at Acme, likes what you have to offer and states that he is in favor of outsourcing the full payroll function to NPC. In fact, they have been close to signing several times, but it seems like some crisis always pops up at the last minute and diverts everyone's attention away from your proposition.

Tony has just called you at the office and requested that you come over to Acme this next week. He indicated that things looked pretty good right now. In fact, as a result of the crisis that left you sitting in the board room alone with an unsigned contract, the company has begun a major acquisition of one of its primary competitors. To handle all the auditing and accounting that the merger requires, Tony needs his full staff. At the same time, annual payroll tax reports are due in about three months and will require a large percentage of his staff's time.

Tony has presented the situation and available options to the various financial officers who would have to sign-off on the outsourcing decision. The response seemed favorable toward NPC's proposal. The only exceptions were two or three individuals who are reluctant to have an outsider handling delicate payroll information. Tony has set the meeting up so that all these individuals can be present. As Tony said right before he ended the phone conversation with you, "I've done everything I can to set it up for you. Now the ball is in your court. Get over here and see what you can do to tie this thing together. I have other fish to fry!"

Harcourt Brace & Company

THE EXERCISE ASSIGNMENT

With this scenario as the basis for your assumptions, use the following worksheet space to develop, explain, and illustrate with examples just how you would use different techniques to gain the commitment of the financial services buying team at Acme.

Method One:

_____

_____

_____

_____

_____

Method Two:

_____

_____

_____

_____

_____

Method Three:

_____

_____

_____

_____

_____

Harcourt Brace & Company

Method Four:

_____

_____

_____

_____

_____

Method Five:

_____

_____

_____

_____

_____

Method Six:

_____

_____

_____

_____

_____

Method Seven:

_____

_____

_____

_____

_____

Harcourt Brace & Company

SKILLS FOR EARNING COMMITMENT
AND NEGOTIATING RESISTANCE
EXPERIENTIAL EXERCISE 11.6
Gaining Commitment—
Discussion Questions

OBJECTIVE: You will be able to understand some of the key issues and roadblocks to gaining commitment.

THE EXERCISE ASSIGNMENT

Please respond to the following statements:

1. How does the kind of product you sell affect when you should attempt to gain commitment?

    _____

    _____

    _____

    _____

2. How would you handle the situation if someone comes into your prospect's office just as you are ready to seek a commitment and he or she stays around?

    _____

    _____

    _____

    _____

Harcourt Brace & Company

3. Why is it natural for the prospect to say "No"?

    _____

    _____

    _____

    _____

4. What would you gain by having the prospect list the disadvantages of buying, when using the T-account?

    _____

    _____

    _____

    _____

Harcourt Brace & Company

SKILLS FOR EARNING COMMITMENT AND NEGOTIATING RESISTANCE
EXPERIENTIAL EXERCISE 11.7
Reasons for Sales Resistance

OBJECTIVE: You will be able to understand the different reasons for sales resistance and how to overcome these barriers.

INTRODUCTION

There are two types of sales resistance: psychological and logical. Psychological resistance refers to an unwillingness to buy based on attitude, emotion, or prejudice. Such resistance is very subjective and varies from one prospect to another. Logical resistance or objections to the sales presentation refers to unwillingness to buy based on tangible considerations related to some aspect of the product.

THE EXERCISE ASSIGNMENT

Following are brief descriptions of the most common types of psychological and logical sales resistance. Write your suggestions for addressing these barriers in the space provided.

Psychological Barriers

1. Resistance to interference: Sales rep's call or visit is viewed as an interruption of what prospect is doing.

    Suggestions for sales reps to overcome this type of resistance:

    _____

    _____

    _____

2. Preference for established habits: Prospect finds comfort in present habits. A purchase usually involves a change in habits.

    Suggestions for sales reps to overcome this type of resistance:

    _____

    _____

    _____

Harcourt Brace & Company

3. Apathy toward product: Prospect feels no need for product, so is unwilling to spend money for it.

   Suggestions for sales reps to overcome this type of resistance:

   _____

   _____

   _____

4. Resistance to giving up something: Prospect views purchase as giving up money in exchange for product.

   Suggestions for sales reps to overcome this type of resistance:

   _____

   _____

   _____

5. Negative stereotype of sales reps: Prospect has feeling of contempt and suspicion toward all sales reps.

   Suggestions for sales reps to overcome this type of resistance:

   _____

   _____

   _____

6. Resistance to domination: Prospect has a need to feel in control of the situation.

   Suggestions for sales reps to overcome this type of resistance:

   _____

   _____

   _____

7. Preconceived ideas about product: Prospect's ideas and feelings, accurate or not, may close his or her mind to the purchase.

   Suggestions for sales reps to overcome this type of resistance:

   _____

   _____

   _____

Harcourt Brace & Company

8. Dislike of making decisions: Prospect may fear consequences of deciding and dread disturbing the status quo. May be due to lack of self-confidence.

Suggestions for sales reps to overcome this type of resistance:

_____

_____

_____

Logical Barriers

When a prospect raises an objection, he or she is signaling the feeling of conflict between buying and not buying the product. A pessimistic sales rep will feel discouraged by objections. The optimistic sales rep will welcome logical objections, realizing they indicate at least some desire to buy.

The specific causes of logical resistance vary from industry to industry, so only the broadest categories will be included here. Later in the session you will develop a list of the specific resistance you encounter in your interactions with prospects.

1. Price: Probably the most frequently cited objection.

Suggestions for sales reps to overcome this type of resistance:

_____

_____

_____

2. Delivery schedule: The importance of delivery time varies with the time-related priorities of the prospect.

Suggestions for sales reps to overcome this type of resistance:

_____

_____

_____

3. Specifications: Drawn up with input from the end user or by the technical experts.

Suggestions for sales reps to overcome this type of resistance:

_____

_____

_____

4. Inadequate warranty

    Suggestions for sales reps to overcome this type of resistance:

    _____

    _____

    _____

5. Does not have feature a competitor has

    Suggestions for sales reps to overcome this type of resistance:

    _____

    _____

    _____

6. Performance does not measure up to the competition

    Suggestions for sales reps to overcome this type of resistance:

    _____

    _____

    _____

7. Other? _____

    Suggestions for sales reps to overcome this type of resistance:

    _____

    _____

    _____

Harcourt Brace & Company

SKILLS FOR EARNING COMMITMENT
AND NEGOTIATING RESISTANCE
EXPERIENTIAL EXERCISE 11.8
*LAARC: A Process for Negotiating
Buyer Resistance*

OBJECTIVE: You will develop your skills in dealing with buyer resistance.

INTRODUCTION

LAARC, an effective process for dealing with sales resistance from a buyer, has been developed in industry training programs. The term *LAARC* is an acronym describing a process for salespeople to follow in working with sales resistance:

- **Listen:** Listen to what the buyer is saying. Avoid the ever-present temptation to anticipate what the buyer is going to say and cut her or him off with a premature response. Learn to listen—it is more than just being polite or professional. The buyer is trying to tell you something that he or she considers important.

- **Acknowledge:** As the buyer completes his or her statement, acknowledge that you received the message and that you appreciate and can understand the concern. Don't jump in with an instantaneous defensive response. Before responding, you need a better understanding about what the buyer is saying. By politely pausing and then simply acknowledging his or her statement, you set yourself up to be a reasonable person—a professional who appreciates other people's opinions. It also buys you precious moments for composing yourself and thinking of questions for the next step.

- **Assess:** This step is similar to assessment in the ADAPT process of questioning. This step in dealing with buyer resistance calls for the salesperson to ask assessment questions to gain a better understanding of exactly *what* the buyer is saying and *why* he or she is saying it. Equipped with this information and understanding, the salesperson is better able to make a meaningful response to the buyer's resistance.

- **Respond:** Based on his or her understanding of what and why the buyer is resisting, the salesperson can respond to the buyer's resistance. Response typically follows the method that is most appropriate for the situation. The more traditional methods for response include: putting off the objection until a more logical time in the presentation, switching focus, using offsetting strategies, using denial, building value, and providing proof.

- **Confirm:** After responding, the salesperson should ask confirmatory questions—response checks to make sure that the buyer's concerns have been adequately met.

Harcourt Brace & Company

Once this is confirmed, the presentation can proceed. In fact, experience indicates that this form of buyer confirmation is often a sufficient buying signal to warrant the salesperson's attempt to gain a commitment.

THE EXERCISE ASSIGNMENT

Using the following worksheet, address each of the indicated buyer objections using the LAARC process. The *Listen* step is implicit and omitted from the written responses. Take time to write out your answers. Responses will be used in class discussion.

Your price is too high.

Acknowledge _____

_____

Assess _____

_____

Respond _____

_____

Confirm _____

_____

I like what I see, but I need to talk with my boss before I do anything.

Acknowledge _____

_____

Assess _____

_____

Respond _____

_____

Confirm _____

_____

Harcourt Brace & Company

I just don't think we need it, we already use your competitor's products and they work all right.

Acknowledge _____

_____

Assess _____

_____

Respond _____

_____

Confirm _____

_____

I'm just not sure our employees can adapt to the new technology.

Acknowledge _____

_____

Assess _____

_____

Respond _____

_____

Confirm _____

_____

The last time we bought from your company we had problems with product reliability.

Acknowledge _____

_____

Assess _____

_____

Respond _____

_____

Confirm _____

_____

Talk to your boss about the warranty and price. See what you can do and get back to me.

Acknowledge _____

_____

Assess _____

_____

Respond _____

_____

Confirm _____

_____

Harcourt Brace & Company

SKILLS FOR EARNING COMMITMENT AND NEGOTIATING RESISTANCE
EXPERIENTIAL EXERCISE 11.9
Negotiating Buyer Resistance

✳

OBJECTIVE: You will develop your skills in recognizing and dealing with different forms of buyer resistance.

THE EXERCISE ASSIGNMENT

At the beginning of this exercise, your instructor will pass out cards to all members of the class. Each card contains a statement or comment that is commonly made by buyers to salespeople. These buyer statements illustrate a wide variety of the different forms of resistance. After reviewing the resistance statement appearing on the card, each member of the class will role-play the part of a salesperson and demonstrate how they would handle the situation while negotiating the specific buyer resistance. Your role-play should:

1. Be conducted within the LAARC framework for working through buyer resistance (as discussed in the introduction to Exercise 11.8)

2. Incorporate a variety of the strategies for responding to buyer resistance that have been discussed in class. Some of the more common strategies are listed below.

COMMONLY USED METHODS FOR NEGOTIATING SALES RESISTANCE

I. Put-Off Strategies

II. Switching Focus Strategies
　　　　　a. Alternative Product
　　　　　b. Feel, Felt, Found
　　　　　c. Comparison and Contrast

III. Offsetting Strategies
　　　　　a. Compensation and Counter-Balance
　　　　　b. Boomerang

Harcourt Brace & Company

IV. Denial Strategies
a. Indirect
b. Direct

V. Handling Price Strategies
a. Build Perceived Value
b. Break Into Smaller Units
c. Price-Value Comparisons
d. Emphasize Uniqueness

VI. Proof Providing Strategies
a. Case Histories
b. Demonstrations
c. Trial Usage

Source: Adapted from an exercise submitted by Jill S. Attaway, Michael A. Humphreys, Timothy A. Longfellow, and Michael R. Williams; Department of Marketing, Illinois State University, (1995).

Harcourt Brace & Company

MODULE TWELVE

SKILLS FOR DEVELOPING AND ENHANCING BUYER–SELLER RELATIONSHIPS

In traditional selling, salespeople too often felt their job was over when they closed the sale. Once the order was obtained, they moved on to the next prospect. Any follow-up or customer service was minimal. The lifeline of an organization today is repeat business. It is important to get new customers but it is critical to keep your existing customer base happy. Not following up with a new customer is a shortsighted attitude toward selling, for it fails to consider the importance of developing and maintaining a customer for your company.

There are several ways you can convert new customers into highly committed lifetime customers: (1) building goodwill by continually adding value to your product, (2) handling complaints in a timely and thoughtful manner, (3) processing requests for rush deliveries yourself and following through until delivery is made, and (4) handling special requests willingly and letting the customer know you will do everything you can to make that request happen.

Those salespeople who over-promise and under-deliver run the risk of having to start the relationship over from the beginning each time they return to a poorly treated customer. Without the benefit of a mutually beneficial buyer–seller relationship, every transaction must be renegotiated.

On the other hand, relationship-oriented salespeople are creating bonds with their customers that will partially isolate them from competitive pressures, or at least minimize the importance of easily altered and matched competitive variables such as price.

Now that you understand the importance of developing and enhancing buyer–seller relationships, Experiential Exercise 12.1 (*The Salesperson as Creator of Added Customer Value*) addresses the issue of people buying people. Your efforts with your buyer will go a long way in determining how the buyer perceives whether you are different from and better than a competitor.

You will have an opportunity in Experiential Exercises 12.2 (*Diary of Sales/Service Encounters*) and 12.3 (*Post-Presentation Follow-up: Analyzing a Sales Call*) to observe actual selling encounters and share these experiences with your classmates. Drawing on,

Harcourt Brace & Company

documenting, and comparing actual selling encounters experienced by your classmates will encourage cognitive involvement and improved understanding of how certain sales behaviors can stimulate or stifle trust in buyer–seller relationships. Further, Experiential Exercise 12.3 offers the opportunity to spend time in the field with a salesperson and critique his or her behaviors in relationship building.

Writing letters can enhance relationships and help the buyer remember your most recent sales call. In Experiential Exercise 12.4 (*Thank-you Letters*) you will write a letter after a sales call to thank a prospect for his or her time. You will also write a letter to a customer who has signed an order to do business with you. A final thank-you letter is written to the buyer of an existing account in which the ordering is automatic. Similarly, in Experiential Exercise 12.5 (*Experiencing the Real World: Registering a Complaint*) you will write a formal letter of complaint regarding a personal buying experience in which expectations were poorly met. Experiential Exercises 12.6 (*What Do You Do If You Don't Gain Commitment?*) and 12.7 (*What to Do after Gaining Commitment*) ask you how to treat customers whether they buy or not. Finally, Experiential Exercise 12.8 (*Enhancing Customer Relationships*) surveys your personal perspective on how to enhance a buyer-seller relationship.

SKILLS FOR DEVELOPING AND ENHANCING BUYER-SELLER RELATIONSHIPS
EXPERIENTIAL EXERCISE 12.1
The Salesperson as Creator of Added Customer Value

OBJECTIVE: You will develop an understanding of the important role played by the salesperson in differentiating a company's market offering by creating added value for the customer.

INTRODUCTION

The boundary-spanning role of salespeople places them in the principal position for creating and sustaining long-term buyer–seller relationships. As such, salespeople represent the keystone in an organization's strategy to achieve competitive advantage through the use of relationship marketing, thereby creating added customer value. These points of added customer value represent significant points for differentiation of a company's market offering.

THE EXERCISE ASSIGNMENT

This exercise explores potential points of added-value differentiation by comparing various facets of the subject company's market offering with those of a principal competitor. Find a salesperson who is willing to be interviewed. After reviewing the *Customer Benefits Worksheet* and *Points for Discussion* following this introduction, interview that salesperson to determine how his or her market offering (including the activities of the salesperson) compares with that of a specific competitor. Determine where the salesperson's offering has an advantage over the competition that results in added customer value. Based on your interview, complete the following *Customer Benefits Worksheet* and *Points for Discussion* pages in your workbook.

Harcourt Brace & Company

Student Name: _____ Date: _____

Name of Salesperson Interviewed: _____

Name of Salesperson's Company: _____

Type of Product: _____

 CUSTOMER BENEFITS WORKSHEET

SOURCE OF BENEFIT	BENEFITS OF COMPANY'S OFFERING	BENEFITS OF COMPETITOR'S OFFERING
THE PRODUCT		
SERVICES		
THE COMPANY		
THE SALESPERSON		

Harcourt Brace & Company

Points for Discussion

1. Describe this salesperson's relationship-marketing role in creating added customer value. What does the salesperson do that adds value for the customer?

_____

_____

_____

_____

_____

_____

_____

_____

2. What additional behaviors or activities, other than those already being performed, could the salesperson undertake that might further increase customer value?

_____

_____

_____

_____

_____

_____

_____

Harcourt Brace & Company

3. Why have these behaviors or services not been implemented?

_____

_____

_____

_____

_____

_____

_____

_____

_____

Harcourt Brace & Company

SKILLS FOR DEVELOPING AND ENHANCING BUYER-SELLER RELATIONSHIPS
EXPERIENTIAL EXERCISE 12.2
Diary of Sales/Service Encounters

OBJECTIVE: You will draw on, document, and compare actual selling encounters to encourage cognitive involvement and improved understanding of how certain sales behaviors can stimulate or stifle trust in buyer–seller relationships.

THE EXERCISE ASSIGNMENT

Part A:
Keeping a Diary of Sales Encounters

Using the following preformatted worksheets, keep a sales/service diary for one month. Include all your encounters with salespeople, recording (1) the date, (2) where the sales encounter happened, (3) a factual description of what happened (that is, the salesperson's attitude, behaviors, and so forth), and (4) your reactions and attitudes (that is, your perceptions, feelings, future intentions).

Part B:
Written Report with
Conclusions/Implications

At the end of one month, select two sales encounters from those in your diary—one encounter that you rate from good to outstanding and one that you rate from poor to terrible. Write a short report comparing the two encounters. Summarize each encounter, assess what went wrong as well as what went right, and develop conclusions and implications for salespeople relevant to relationship selling.

Part C:
Oral Presentation and Discussion

Based on your written report, prepare and deliver an oral presentation to the class. This oral presentation should be informative and emphasize your conclusions and implications for relationship selling.

Adapted from Leonard L. Berry, "Educational Perspectives of Relationship Marketing," 1994 AMA Faculty Consortium, Emory University, Atlanta, Georgia, 1994.

Harcourt Brace & Company

Student Name: _____ Date: _____

Diary of Sales/Service Encounters

Encounter	Date	Where	What Happened/Behaviors	Your Reactions/Attitudes
1.				
2.				
3.				
4.				
5.				
6.				

Harcourt Brace & Company

Harcourt Brace & Company

ENCOUNTER	DATE	WHERE	WHAT HAPPENED/BEHAVIORS	YOUR REACTIONS/ATTITUDES
7.				
8.				
9.				
10.				
11.				
12.				

continued on next page

ENCOUNTER	DATE	WHERE	WHAT HAPPENED/BEHAVIORS	YOUR REACTIONS/ATTITUDES
13.				
14.				
15.				
16.				
17.				
18.				

Harcourt Brace & Company

Harcourt Brace & Company

Encounter	Date	Where	What Happened/Behaviors	Your Reactions/Attitudes
19.				
20.				
21.				
22.				
23.				
24.				

SKILLS FOR DEVELOPING AND ENHANCING BUYER-SELLER RELATIONSHIPS
EXPERIENTIAL EXERCISE 12.3
Post-Presentation Follow-up: Analyzing a Sales Call

OBJECTIVE: You will be able to analyze the sales call of a salesperson during a shadow call.

THE EXERCISE ASSIGNMENT

After you have shadowed a salesperson on a sales call, you will be able to evaluate the strengths and weaknesses of the call by responding to the following questions.

1. What might the salesperson have done better? _____

    _____

    _____

2. What did the salesperson say or do that they wish they had not? _____

    _____

    _____

3. Did the salesperson discuss topics that were not relevant to the sale? _____

    _____

    _____

    _____

4. Did the salesperson venture into subjects that could have led to an argument?

    _____

    _____

    _____

Harcourt Brace & Company

5. Did the salesperson's talk stray from the purpose at hand? _____

_____

_____

6. Did the salesperson talk too much? _____

_____

_____

7. Did the salesperson detect the prospect becoming weary when points were belabored?

_____

_____

_____

8. Did the salesperson interrupt or cut the customer off during the discussion?

_____

_____

_____

9. Was the presentation too one-sided? _____

_____

_____

10. How could the sale have been increased? _____

_____

_____

11. Could the salesperson's presentation have been more persuasive and the sales results better?

_____

_____

_____

Harcourt Brace & Company

12. Did the salesperson listen to what the customer had to say? _____

_____

_____

13. Did the salesperson present the product in terms of customer needs?

_____

_____

_____

14. As the salesperson talked, was he or she thinking of the customer?

_____

_____

_____

15. Were the suggested applications interesting to the customer? _____

_____

_____

_____

16. Whose real interest did the salesperson have in mind? _____

_____

_____

17. Will the salesperson be welcome on the next call to this customer?

_____

_____

_____

SKILLS FOR DEVELOPING AND ENHANCING BUYER-SELLER RELATIONSHIPS
EXPERIENTIAL EXERCISE 12.4
Thank-You Letters

OBJECTIVE: You will increase your awareness of the important, effective, and efficient role played by thank-you letters in customer follow-up while gaining practice in writing thank-you letters.

THE EXERCISE ASSIGNMENT

Visualize yourself as a salesperson for Montgomery Paper Products, one of the top three firms in business supplies, paper, and paper products. Today has been a very hectic day, but one that you feel has been productive nevertheless. You have just returned to your office from calling on John Tracy, the head buyer for Worldwide Systems, Inc.

Worldwide currently sources all their paper needs from Acme Office Products. However, Acme has failed to keep Worldwide current on several technological advances. The fact that Montgomery Paper Products is the innovator and pioneer for several of these technological advances gives you an advantage in the marketplace. You have been using the potential benefits this new technology would produce for Worldwide as leverage to gain access to a portion of Worldwide's business.

Although John recognizes the benefits of changing to your line of products, he still has some reservations regarding your products being compatible with his existing equipment. You have been chipping away at this account for several months now. In fact, today's call is the sixth time you have met with John and other interested parties over at Worldwide. Even though they continue to express interest and ask that you keep them informed, they still have not committed to a purchase. Nevertheless, you sense they are moving closer.

Part One:

Using the following worksheet, compose a thank-you letter to John Tracy for his consideration in visiting with you today. You never know—a small act of professionalism might just be the one event that gets you the sale. Besides, the letter gives you an opportunity to get your name and product benefits in front of him one more time.

Harcourt Brace & Company

MONTGOMERY PAPER PRODUCTS

1800 Eastport Road   Chicago, IL 63984   (715) 756-8333

Part Two:

Visualize the same scenario, except that you did get the order you were after. Not only that, John indicated that if you and Montgomery Paper Products carry through and do what you say you will do, there is strong potential for added business. How would your thank-you letter differ from that in the earlier scenario? Compose this new letter in the space below:

MONTGOMERY PAPER PRODUCTS
1800 Eastport Road   Chicago, IL 63984   (715) 756-8333

Part Three:

Now for the hard one. Suppose the scenario is changed and Montgomery Paper is the primary supplier for Worldwide. You still service the account and John is the buyer. You still call on John, but you also spend a lot of time working with the people in the office and shop who actually use your products. In fact, relations are so good that most of the ordering is automatic. How would this letter look? Compose it in the space below:

MONTGOMERY PAPER PRODUCTS

1800 Eastport Road   Chicago, IL 63984   (715) 756-8333

Harcourt Brace & Company

SKILLS FOR DEVELOPING AND ENHANCING BUYER–SELLER RELATIONSHIPS
EXPERIENTIAL EXERCISE 12.5
Experiencing the Real World: Registering a Complaint

OBJECTIVE: You will write a letter of complaint to a company in which your expectations were poorly met. You will better understand how businesses go about handling such complaints.

THE EXERCISE ASSIGNMENT

Write a formal letter of complaint regarding a personal buying experience in which your expectations were poorly met. Later, present your complaint letter in class and discuss the company response you received, if any.

What were your attitudes and intentions regarding this firm before writing your letter?

_____

_____

_____

_____

_____

_____

_____

Adapted from Leonard L. Berry, "Educational Perspectives of Relationship Marketing," 1994 AMA Faculty Consortium, Emory University, Atlanta, Georgia, 1994.

Harcourt Brace & Company

SKILLS FOR DEVELOPING AND ENHANCING BUYER-SELLER RELATIONSHIPS
EXPERIENTIAL EXERCISE 12.6
What Do You Do If You Don't Gain Commitment?

OBJECTIVE: You will discover that a prospect's No may be the beginning of building the relationship.

THE EXERCISE ASSIGNMENT

In the role of a salesperson calling on your school's purchasing department, the buyer has just informed you that they have made the buying decision in favor of your competitor. What do you do now? Please respond to the following questions.

1. Thank the prospect for his or her time. Why? _____

    _____

    _____

    _____

    _____

2. Request permission to call again. Why? _____

    _____

    _____

    _____

    _____

3. Provide the prospect information through regular future mailings and/or calls. Why?

_____

_____

_____

_____

4. Avoid showing disappointment, conveying a feeling of defeat, or expressing anger over perceived unfair treatment. Why?

_____

_____

_____

_____

5. Offer your assistance in solving future problems. Create the mindset that interacting with you in the future would be a positive, beneficial, and natural thing to do. Why?

_____

_____

_____

_____

Harcourt Brace & Company

SKILLS FOR DEVELOPING AND ENHANCING BUYER-SELLER RELATIONSHIPS
EXPERIENTIAL EXERCISE 12.7
What to Do after Gaining Commitment

OBJECTIVE: The sales rep has to complete a number of activities once the order has been signed. You will understand what activities must be completed after earning commitment.

THE EXERCISE ASSIGNMENT

In the role of a salesperson calling on your school's purchasing department, the buyer has just informed you that they have made the buying decision in your favor. What do you do now? Please respond to the following questions.

1. Confirm the customer's decision. How do you accomplish this?

   _____

   _____

   _____

2. Show appreciation. How do you accomplish this?

   _____

   _____

   _____

3. Cement the relationship. How do you accomplish this?

   _____

   _____

   _____

4. Monitor delivery. How do you accomplish this?

   _____

   _____

   _____

Harcourt Brace & Company

5. Monitor installation. How do you accomplish this?

_____

_____

_____

6. Keep your promises. How do you accomplish this?

_____

_____

_____

7. Handle complaints with sensitivity. How do you accomplish this?

_____

_____

_____

8. Respect the customer's time. How do you accomplish this?

_____

_____

_____

9. Provide information on the care and use of products. How do you accomplish this?

_____

_____

_____

10. List some specific follow-up actions that will cement the relationship between you and your customers.

_____

_____

_____

Harcourt Brace & Company

SKILLS FOR DEVELOPING AND ENHANCING BUYER-SELLER RELATIONSHIPS
EXPERIENTIAL EXERCISE 12.8
Enhancing Customer Relationships

OBJECTIVE: You will be able to understand that building mutually satisfying relationships between buyers and sellers is essential for success in sales.

THE EXERCISE ASSIGNMENT

To build mutually satisfying relationships between buyers and sellers, professional salespeople must be competent in accomplishing five ongoing tasks:

1. Provide information. What does this mean and why is it important to building a relationship?

    _____

    _____

    _____

    _____

2. Reduce risk. What does this mean and why is it important to building a relationship?

    _____

    _____

    _____

    _____

Harcourt Brace & Company

3. Establish high standards and expectations. What does this mean and why is it important to building a relationship?

    _____

    _____

    _____

    _____

4. Anticipate and respond to customer problems and concerns. What does this mean and why is it important to building a relationship?

    _____

    _____

    _____

    _____

5. Monitor and improve customer satisfaction. What does this mean and why is it important to building a relationship?

    _____

    _____

    _____

    _____

Harcourt Brace & Company

CREDITS

Exercise 01.01	Adapted from *A Call for Action: Students Assessment of Personal Selling*, A.J. Dubinsky, Unpublished Working Paper #27 (University of Minnesota), December 1977; and *The Impact of Classroom Style on Student Attitudes Toward Sales Careers: A Comparative Approach*, R.R. Lagace and T.A. Longfellow (JOURNAL OF MARKETING EDUCATION, Fall 1989).
Table 02.01	K.J. Corcoran, L.K. Peterson, D.B. Baitch, M.R Barrett, *High Performance Sales Organizations: Creating Competitive Advantage in the Global Marketplace*, Irwin ©1995, p. 50.
Exercise 02.01	Adapted with permission from CERTIFICATION STUDY GUIDE ©Copyright Sales and Marketing Executives International and Thomas N. Ingram, CSE, Ph.D.
Table 02.02	Adapted from S.X. Doyle and G.T. Roth, *Selling and Sales Management in Action: The Use of Insight and Coaching to Improve Relationship Selling*, JOURNAL OF PERSONAL SELLING AND SALES MANAGEMENT (Winter 1992, p. 62)
Exercise 02.03	Adapted from: Trawick, Swan, McGee, and Rink, JOURNAL OF THE ACADEMY OF MARKETING SCIENCE (Vol.19 No.1) pp. 17–23; Dubinsky and Ingram, *Correlates of Salespeople Ethical Conflict: An Exploratory Investigation*, JOURNAL OF BUSINESS ETHICS (1984) pp. 343–353; Dubinsky and Gwin, *Business Ethics: Buyers and Sellers*, JOURNAL OF PURCHASING AND MATERIALS MANAGEMENT (Vol. 17, Winter 1981) pp. 9–16
Exercise 02.04	Adapted from: Trawick, Swan, McGee, and Rink, JOURNAL OF THE ACADEMY OF MARKETING SCIENCE (Vol. 19 No.1) pp. 17–23; Dubinsky and Ingram, *Correlates of Salespeople Ethical Conflict: An Exploratory Investigation*, JOURNAL OF BUSINESS ETHICS (1984) pp.343–353; Dubinsky and Gwin, *Business Ethics: Buyers and Sellers*, JOURNAL OF PURCHASING AND MATERIALS MANAGEMENT (Vol. 17, Winter 1981) pp. 9–16.
Exercise 02.05	Adapted from an exercise submitted for use in this textbook by T.A. Longfellow and M.R. Williams, Illinois State University.
Table 03.02	Tony Alessandra, Phil Wexler, and Rick Barrera, *Non–Manipulative Selling*, ©1987, p. 7. Adapted by permission of Prentice Hall, Upper Saddle River, NJ.
Exercise 04.01	Used with permission from CERTIFICATION STUDY GUIDE © Copyright Sales and Marketing Executives International and Thomas N. Ingram, CSE, Ph.D.
Exercise 05.02	Adapted from an exercise submitted for use in this textbook by M.R.Luthy, Assistant Professor of Marketing, Drake University, Des Moines, Iowa.
Exercise 05.03	Source: Camille Schuster, Professor of Marketing, Xavier University.
Exercise 05.04	Source: Camille Schuster, Professor of Marketing, Xavier University.
Exercise 05.05	Gerald L. Manning and Barry L. Reece, *Selling Today: An Extension of the Marketing Concept*, © 1995, p. 86–94. Adapted by permission of Prentice Hall, Upper Saddle River, NJ.
Exercise 06.02	Adapted from *The Soft Sell*, Tom Connor (T.R. Training Associates) pp. 64–66
Exercise 06.05	Adapted from an exercise submitted for use in this textbook by Donald McBane and Patricia A. Knocks, Clemson University.

Exercise 06.06   Adapted from an exercise submitted for use in this textbook by Donald McBane and Patricia A. Knocks, Clemson University.

Exercise 07.05   Source: Camille Schuster, Professor of Marketing, Xavier University.

Exercise 07.06   Source: *Instructor's Manual to Accompany Selling Principles and Methods* by Carlton A. Pederson, Milburne D. Wright, and Barton Weitz (Irwin, 1983)

Exercise 09.04   Adapted with permission from CERTIFICATION STUDY GUIDE © Copyright Sales and Marketing Executives International and Thomas N. Ingram, CSE, Ph.D.

Exercise 10.03   Adapted from *A Tiger's Guide to Professional Selling Course Packet*, D.A. McBane and P.A. Knowles, Department of Marketing, Clemson University (1994); and *Sales Presentation Planning Report*, J.S. Attaway, M.A. Humphreys, T.A. Longfellow, and M.R. Williams, Department of Marketing, Illinois State University (1994).

Exercise 10.04   Adapted from *The Soft Sell*, Tom Connor (T.R. Training Associates) pp. 101, 124–125

Exercise 11.02   Adapted from: *Selling Selling Sold*, David Seigal (Kendall Hunt Publishing Co., 1985) p. 208; *The Best Seller: The American Management Association*, D.F. Ley (Sales Success Press, 1986) p. 110; and *The Professional Selling Process*, John C. Haffer (West Publishing Company, 1993) p. 165.

Exercise 11.03   Adapted from *Selling Selling Sold*, David Seigel (Kendall Hunt Publishing Co., 1985) p. 165.

Exercise 11.07   Adapted from *The Handbook of Selling Psychological, Managerial, and Marketing Bases*, Gary M. Grikscheit, Harold C. Cash, W.J.E. Crissy (John Wiley and Sons, Inc., 1981) pp. 139–146.

Exercise 12.02   Adapted from *Educational Perspectives of Relationship Marketing*, Leonard L. Berry (1994 AMA Faculty Consortium).

Exercise 12.03   Adapted from *Creative Selling*, H.W. Johnson and A.J. Faria (Southwestern Publishing Company, 1993) p. 322.

Exercise 12.05   Adapted from *Educational Perspectives of Relationship Marketing*, Leonard L. Berry (1994 AMA Faculty Consortium).

Exercise 12.08   Adapted from *Selling Building Partnerships*, B.A. Weits, S.A. Castleberry, J.F. Tanner (Irwin, 1992) pp. 316–318.